Praise for *The Art of C*

T0278749

"*The Art of Clear Thinking* pulls yo
fighter jet. Entertaining and profound . . . Hasard takes you
on a heart-pounding journey through life-or-death stories
woven with the critical decision-making tips taught to elite
fighter pilots. This book will sharpen your ability to stop,
see clearly, and make the key choices that may change the
entire course of your future."

—Harvey Karp, world-renowned pediatrician,
creator of Happiest Baby, Inc., and bestselling author

"Hasard's great service with this book is to put the reader in
the seat of fifth-generation fighter pilots, the world's foremost
laboratory for high-pressure, high-consequence human decisions, and then share their sophisticated and proven decision
insights in an easy-to-read-and-apply manner. All with stories
that take place at Mach speed and will have you turning the
page. As someone who spent decades leading special operations and pursuing high-risk sports like BASE jumping and
speed flying, but also as a business entrepreneur, I've incorporated Hasard's incredibly valuable decision-making tools into
the complex world I experience daily, and you will too."

—Dan Schilling, Spec Ops Commander, decorated Black Hawk
Down veteran, and *New York Times* bestselling author

"As a former fighter pilot with two tours in Vietnam, I loved
this book. For over a hundred years, aerial combatants have
shared their death-defying stories. The examples Hasard
shares, though, are more than simply exciting flying stories.
When he describes rolling in with his gun and raining down
one hundred rounds per second on the bad guys to save U.S.

lives, it's not simply for braggadocio. It helps readers learn about resourcefulness and planning when lives are on the line. And it also helps the executive to deal with adversity in a fluid situation when millions of dollars are at stake in the C-suite. This book is replete with examples from aviation and industry that will help you to make better decisions. I relished reading this book and wholeheartedly recommend it without reservation."

—George Nolly, 315 combat missions, twenty-four
Air Medals, three Distinguished Flying Crosses, and author

"This book brought me right back to my days flying fighters, but also to my time in space. I couldn't put it down. Even more than the heart-pounding fighter pilot stories, Hasard has some powerful and practical words of wisdom for any leader, on Earth or in space."

—Terry Virts, Space Station Commander,
NASA astronaut, test pilot, and author

"As a former CIA intelligence officer, I place a premium value on processes that enable you to make quick decisions—to manage chaos, mitigate risk, and employ sound judgment under the most stressful conditions. In Hasard's book, we learn from the best—an F-35 fighter pilot and trainer—the intricacies of how to make sound decisions on the fly. Decision-making is such a critical life skill, yet one rarely taught to the general public, until now. Hasard's well-honed decision-making process can transform your operations and output, giving you the advantage in a world full of uncertainty and risk."

—Michele Rigby Assad, former undercover
CIA agent and author

"Strap in and hold on as Hasard Lee lights the afterburner on leadership and risk management under extreme pressure. *The Art of Clear Thinking* is a riveting read, full of instantly actionable advice—not just for high-stakes decisions, but also for handling everyday choices at work and home."

—Scott Parazynski, five-time NASA Space Shuttle veteran, Astronaut Hall of Fame, physician, and author

"Hasard's book will be transformative for artists, business-people, and creative entrepreneurs of all backgrounds. As an artist, I've witnessed how true creativity is forged from crucible moments, and Hasard is an expert on this topic. His stories paint vivid visuals of split-second life-and-death decisions. They transport you into the cockpit of a full-throttle F-35 fighter jet galloping across the sky at twelve hundred miles per hour, when every minor mistake or deviation could end in fiery oblivion. Do you have the strength to handle such stress? Most human beings would quickly crumble into fine Sonoran desert sand. Luckily for you, Hasard can be your coach and guide with this book—page by page, generously sharing his hard-earned secrets, and making you stronger, more confident, faster, wiser."

—Drue Kataoka, renowned artist and technologist, and creator of the first art exhibit in space

"Flying a hundred million dollars' worth of state secrets over enemy territory at more than a thousand miles per hour takes a lot of guts, but most people don't realize that just *getting there*, climbing into that cockpit, takes a huge amount of trust. Fighter pilots don't have the benefit of direct oversight;

they have to make critical decisions in fractions of a second, using only the information at hand, and the stakes can often be higher than just life or death. One bad decision behind the stick of an advanced fighter, and you could throw your entire nation into conflict.

"But this book from F-35 pilot Hasard Lee demonstrates with crystal clarity that making the right call isn't a matter of chance; it's a matter of process. It doesn't matter if you're flying a combat mission over Iraq or taking a Zoom meeting from your home office—Hasard's methodical approach to assessing your options, making a call, and owning your outcomes will have you thinking like a fighter pilot, and making mission like one too.

"Born out of scientific analysis, real combat experience, and fighter pilot culture, Hasard pulls the decision-making skills that *make* a fighter pilot out of the cockpit and places them in your hands, providing real-world examples from his experiences flying America's most advanced jets alongside practical examples of these same principles being leveraged in far more grounded business and commercial settings. Aviation lovers will revel in Hasard's first-person accounts of flying incredible aircraft, but literally everyone can benefit from this crash course in decision-making."

—Alex Hollings, editor in chief of *Sandboxx News*

THE ART OF CLEAR THINKING

A Stealth Fighter Pilot's Timeless Rules
for Making Tough Decisions

HASARD LEE

ST. MARTIN'S GRIFFIN
NEW YORK

Published in the United States by St. Martin's Griffin,
an imprint of St. Martin's Publishing Group

THE ART OF CLEAR THINKING. Copyright © 2023 by Justin Lee. All rights
reserved. Printed in the United States of America. For information, address
St. Martin's Publishing Group, 120 Broadway, New York, NY 10271.

www.stmartins.com

Designed by Steven Seighman

The Library of Congress has cataloged the hardcover edition as follows:

Names: Lee, Hasard, author.
Title: The art of clear thinking : a stealth fighter pilot's timeless rules
   for making tough decisions / Hasard Lee.
Description: First edition. | New York : St. Martin's Press, [2023]
Identifiers: LCCN 2023002003 | ISBN 9781250281449 (hardcover) |
   ISBN 9781250281456 (ebook)
Subjects: LCSH: Decision making. | Problem solving.
Classification: LCC HD30.23 .L4196 2023 | DDC 658.4/03—
   dc23/eng/20230118
LC record available at https://lccn.loc.gov/2023002003

ISBN 978-1-250-84585-6 (trade paperback)

Our books may be purchased in bulk for promotional, educational,
or business use. Please contact your local bookseller or the
Macmillan Corporate and Premium Sales Department at 1-800-221-7945,
extension 5442, or by email at MacmillanSpecialMarkets@macmillan.com.

First St. Martin's Griffin Edition: 2024

10 9 8 7 6 5 4 3 2

This book is dedicated to the warriors of the air who've sacrificed their lives for their country and the pursuit of excellence. Nickel on the grass . . .

CONTENTS

INTRODUCTION

As a fighter pilot, one of the things you get used to is always being seconds away from a fiery death. You're balancing on a razor's edge of performance, where the success of each flight hinges on the accumulation of thousands of correct decisions. It only takes one wrong move for a flight to end in catastrophe, which, unfortunately, has happened often throughout our history.

To give you a sense of the speed at which these aircraft can fly, let me share a story from my time in an F-16. I was stationed in Korea, and there was a jet coming out of maintenance—the engine had been swapped out, and they needed a pilot to ensure it was airworthy. It was a clean jet—none of the typical missiles, bombs, targeting pod, or external fuel tanks were loaded. In effect, it was a stripped-down hot rod capable of its theoretical maximum speed.

When we fly, we usually go out as a formation to work on tactics; every drop of fuel is used to prepare for combat. This mission, however, called for me to launch by myself and test the engine at multiple altitudes and power settings, with the final check being a maximum speed run, where I was to push the aircraft to its limit.

After I took off, I entered the designated airspace over the ocean and quickly ran through the various engine checks. Topped off, I could only carry seven thousand pounds of fuel, which is never enough with the giant engine behind me burning tens of thousands of pounds of fuel per hour. If you look at an F-16 from the side, you can see that it's all engine— the structure is built around it, with the pilot sitting atop it at the front.

After fifteen minutes, I had finished all the checks except the last one: the max speed run. I was at twenty-five thousand feet when I pushed the throttle forward until it hit the stop— this was full power from the turbofan. Fighter aircraft, though, have an additional power source called *afterburner*. To enable it, I rotated the throttle outward, allowing me to push it along a separate track. This activated all the boost pumps in the fuel system, which began pulling fuel at a rate that could empty a swimming pool in minutes. This fuel, however, wasn't fed into the engine but rather, like a flamethrower, injected directly into my exhaust and ignited, creating a thirty-foot flame out the back of my aircraft. I could feel the surge in thrust as it pinned me to the back of my seat. I quickly accelerated past Mach 1—the speed of sound that Chuck Yeager famously broke in his Bell X-1. I then began a climb, and within seconds, thirty-five thousand feet went by as I continued to accelerate. Soon I was at forty-five thousand feet, and I began to shallow my climb to arrive at the fifty-thousand-foot service ceiling.

This was as high as I could go, not because the jet couldn't go higher but because if the cockpit depressurized, I would black out within seconds.

Looking out of the canopy at fifty thousand feet, the sky was now noticeably darker—I was above most of the atmosphere and could see the deep shade of indigo above me slowly transition into the ice-blue horizon. The curvature of the earth was also clearly visible as it bowed across my field of view. To my right, I could see the entire Korean peninsula, green with a thin layer of haze over it. To my left, a few clouds over the Yellow Sea separated me from mainland China.

As I maintained my altitude, the jet continued to accelerate. I was now at Mach 1.4, over one thousand miles per hour. I only had a few minutes of fuel left, so to increase my acceleration, I pushed the stick forward and started a dive. Through my heads-up display, I could see Mach 1.5 tick by, backed up by an old analog airspeed gauge in front of me slowly winding clockwise toward the red "never exceed" limit.

At Mach 1.6, the jet began shaking: The extreme stress of the air resistance—over three hundred times what a car experiences at highway speeds—began causing the aluminum-alloy wings to flutter, sending vibrations throughout the plane. They were rapidly increasing at a rate that was not sustainable to the airframe.

AVIATION

To make an aircraft fly is a constant struggle against physics. An airliner traveling six hundred miles per hour at thirty thousand feet is not something that happens naturally. It's not a fail-safe act, meaning the default is to crash—it's up to our ingenuity and decision-making to prevent it from happening. It's a unique environment that's highly unforgiving. Whereas a loss of power in a car typically results in a few hours on the side of a road, a loss of power in the air is often disastrous. Even in business, bet-the-company decisions are rare, and when encountered, only a fraction of the employees take part in them. Aviation, however, relies on everyone performing at an optimum level *just* to keep the aircraft flying. It's an unstable system where even a single person forgetting to do their job, or doing it improperly, can lead to catastrophic results. It was this unforgiving nature, however, that led to a deep focus on decision-making.

In the early days of aviation, it seemed as though the obstacles were insurmountable. The crash rate was incredibly high: Accounting for the number of flights today, there would have been a staggering *seven thousand* airline crashes per year in the late 1920s. This led to a near obsessive culture around increasing the safety of aviation. Anytime an airplane crashed, an investigation was launched to develop lessons that could be incorporated in future flights. It was this unforgiving nature of aviation that provided the perfect framework for analyzing decisions. The spectacular nature of crashes meant they couldn't be brushed aside. After each crash, a team would be sent to find the root cause along with the contributing factors to figure out not only how the airplane crashed but *why*. It was this culture of acknowledging, understanding, and fixing mistakes that eventually enabled the success of the commercial aviation industry. Today it represents one of the great human achievements where, despite nearly one hundred thousand flights taking off per day, U.S. airlines haven't had a single fatal crash in more than a decade.

Air combat adds another layer of complexity to aviation. Not only do pilots have to fly their aircraft safely and contend with weather, terrain, and traffic, among other threats, but they also must compete with an enemy who is trying to shoot them down. The enemy is often highly skilled and adaptable, constantly seeking to exploit vulnerabilities in their opponents' tactics and technology. Each side seeks to deceive and mislead the other in order to interfere with their decision-making ability.

In air combat, the threats are continually changing as each side postures to protect their vulnerabilities while also exploiting their adversary's. Decisions are continually tested and countered in the ultimate cat-and-mouse game. This continual evolution has led to a modern battlefield that is as diverse as it is dangerous.

Today, the enemy is elusive, hiding in the air, on land, in the sea, in space, and within the cyber realm looking to specifically target vulnerabilities. There are hypersonic missiles that can travel over a mile per second, stealth aircraft that look smaller than a hummingbird on radar, and sensors that can triangulate targets out to the horizon. Often, the only warning of an impending attack is the deafening shriek of a weapon just seconds before it impacts. The margin of error is incredibly thin. Every aspect of these planes is skewed toward performance, often at the expense of safety. Coupled with near-unlimited budgets that can climb into the trillions of dollars, this makes for amazingly capable yet dangerous aircraft to fly.

SPEED

As I accelerated past 1.6 times the speed of sound, the jet continued shaking from the stress of the airflow across the wings and fuselage. Looking over my shoulder, I could see the F-16's normally rigid wings bending back and forth in the airstream. I had never been this fast before, nor had I experienced high-speed wing flutter. Although the F-16 was designed for this speed, that was for a brand-new jet off the line, not the one I was flying, which was twenty-five years old with thousands of hours on the airframe. After so many flights, each jet had unique characteristics that we tracked and referenced before every flight.

Unlike previous generations of fighter pilots who each had their own aircraft assigned to them, pilots today all share the jets within a squadron. It's our job to quickly adapt to each jet's unique strengths and weaknesses and merge ourselves into a lethal team. Because a maximum speed run is so rare, there wasn't any data available for this flight—I would have to assess in real time and adapt to the changing conditions.

As the buffeting continued to increase, I began by assessing the situation. Looking through the heads-up display, I could see that I was traveling at Mach 1.6. To rule out the chance that it was indicator error and that I was potentially overspeeding the aircraft, I looked at my standby airspeed gauge and confirmed that my displayed airspeed was correct.

From there, I looked at the sideslip indicator, which told me if my rudder was aligned into the airstream. When it's not properly set, the plane will skid through the sky, causing a decrease in performance. For a max speed run, everything needed to be perfectly aligned. It was slightly off, so I took my hand from the throttle and reached back to the almost-never-used trim panel located behind the seat. I kept my eyes forward—even if I wanted to look at the panel, I wouldn't have been able to see it. The F-16 was designed for a pilot who was five feet, ten inches. Being six feet, two inches, wearing a bulky survival vest and an anti-exposure dry suit to protect myself from the frigid water, I was wedged in the cockpit. I couldn't turn around and see the switches behind me—instead, I had memorized their location and adjusted them by feel.

After centering the rudder, nothing happened. The vibrations were still there and worsening. This was not sustainable to the airframe—an abrupt fatigue failure would be catastrophic at these speeds, causing the plane to instantly break up into thousands of pieces. I was also well outside the ejection envelope; if forced to eject, as soon as the rocket-powered seat blasted me out of the cockpit, nearly every bone in my body would break as it entered the 1,200-mile-per-hour airstream.

I remembered back to a conversation I'd had several years prior with an old fighter pilot who went by the call sign Cygon. At the time, I was just learning how to fly the F-16. Cygon, however, was an experienced fighter pilot who had just finished a staff tour at the Pentagon and was now getting requalified on the F-16. We were both students, although his was just a temporary title before he moved on to lead a combat squadron. Cygon was a fighter pilot's fighter pilot, and despite his high rank and status, he spent time with the students doing the grunt work around the squadron. He was a mentor to the students and even to many of the instructor pilots. This lack of hierarchy allowed us to freely have conversations with him where he would explain the nuances of different tactics and what it took to be a good fighter pilot.

One day I walked into the secure vault, which is the tactical nerve center of every fighter squadron, and Cygon was there telling a story about the test program he had been a part of in the F-16. He had learned that in a clean configuration, the F-16 would begin to buffet at around Mach 1.6—it was a known area where the aerodynamic forces would compound and amplify the vibrations. He said that it was possible to push through it by counterintuitively going *faster*. The change in resonance would dampen the flexing and reduce the vibration. It was an interesting story, but one that I didn't think would apply to the tactical flying we did during day-to-day operations.

By the time I took off on my maximum speed run, I had long since forgotten Cygon's story. However, I've always been amazed at how long-forgotten information can instantly come to you when there's a life-or-death decision to make. Nearly every fighter pilot who's had to eject talks about the clarity they had on the complex sequence of memorized steps they needed to take to be rescued regardless of the time that had passed since their training. As soon as my wings began buffeting, Cygon's story quickly came back to me.

While the overall choice I had to make was only whether to slow down or speed up, each course of action led to further decisions. If I elected to slow down, should I pull out of my dive, adding additional stress to the wings, and if so, how hard? Or should I maintain my current dive and just pull the throttle out of afterburner, which would take longer to slow down but minimize the stress? And if I chose to speed up, should I maintain my dive and reduce my control inputs, or should I increase my dive angle to accelerate faster? There were an infinite number of options on how I could execute my decision.

I didn't have time to think through each option, so I fell back on the mantra, "There's no problem so bad you can't make it worse." The default decision was to leave the aircraft in its current setting. Based on Cygon's story, the vibrations were most likely tied to my current airspeed. I needed to accelerate through that speed as quickly as possible while not putting unnecessary stress on the aircraft. I elected to slowly push forward on the stick, steepening my dive to increase my acceleration while making sure not to add undue stress to the flight controls.

In my heads-up display, I read Mach 1.7 as the vibrations continued to get worse. It now felt like I was driving at highway speeds on an old dirt road. As Mach 1.8 ticked by, it became difficult to read the displays. At this point, my senses were now hyperaware of everything that was happening around me. I could feel a knot in my stomach—maybe I had made the wrong choice. If the plane broke up, nothing of me would be recovered once my body turned into jelly. I quickly pushed the thought away so that I could focus on flying the jet.

Then, at Mach 1.9, everything smoothed out—it became eerily calm as my airspeed crossed 1,500 miles per hour. When flying a fighter, you typically don't have time to enjoy the view—you're in a tactical bubble where your only thought is on the next decision you have to make. This was one of the rare moments where time seemed to slow down, allowing me to take in the experience. Looking down, I could see cargo ships dragging their long wakes across the ocean as they rapidly fell aft of my flight path. I noticed the cockpit felt warm—not like the temperature had been increased but a radiating heat. The friction of the air was causing the skin of the aircraft to rapidly heat. I took my hand off the throttle and put my Nomex glove about a foot away from the canopy and could feel the heat passing through it, like I was sticking my hand in an open oven.

As I entered the thicker atmosphere, my airspeed continued increasing until I was right at the structural limit of the aircraft. Nearly out of fuel and with the max speed run complete, I pulled the throttle out of afterburner. Despite a large amount of thrust still coming from the engine, the drag from the thick air caused the jet to rapidly decelerate, slamming me forward so hard that it locked my shoulder-harness straps. Still, it took nearly fifty miles for the aircraft to decelerate below the sound barrier.

DECISIONS

Boiled down, a fighter pilot's job is to make decisions—thousands of them each flight, often with incomplete information and lives on the line. The decisions start during the mission-planning phase where processes are developed and resources allocated to accomplish an objective. This often involves hundreds of people coming together from disparate backgrounds to align toward one common goal. Then the flight must be executed under the fog and friction of war, where no matter how well a mission is planned, it will change. This means that despite the immense effort that is put into planning a mission, there will always be difficult decisions that need to be made in the air that haven't been anticipated or that don't have textbook answers. Afterward, each decision must then be analyzed to glean any lessons that can be used to improve future decisions.

As fighter pilots, we've been at the leading edge of decision-making theory since Air Force Colonel John Boyd developed the OODA—observe, orient, decide, act—loop based on his experiences flying missions during the Korean War. In the years since, other fighter pilot greats, such as Colonel John Warden and General David Deptula, have made significant contributions to the field. It's a constantly evolving field that gives fighter pilots the best mental tools possible to solve the problems they encounter. Though we have talented pilots, the mantra that we bet our lives on is that a good pilot uses superior judgment to avoid situations that require the use of superior skill. Clean and clear decision-making will nearly always beat talent alone.

The ability to make a correct decision with incomplete information and a limited amount of time is not just for fighter pilots, though—it's a universal skill. From leaders to entrepreneurs to teachers to nurses to first responders, our success and ability to achieve our goals relies on making the right decisions at the right time. The world is a complex adaptive system where all decisions are interconnected—like the gears in a mechanical watch, each decision affects peripheral decisions, often leading to disproportionate changes in outcome. Everything in life is a trade-off; there is a cost—be it time, money, energy, or some other precious resource—for each decision we make. The key is to find the best long-term value for the given cost. And today, the stakes for our decisions have never been higher.

Technology has now automated many of our lower-level tasks. This has added leverage to each decision we make. The computer that I'm typing on can, by itself, perform the job of dozens of people from just a few decades ago, a car can travel over ten times faster than a horse-drawn wagon, a modern combine harvester can harvest crops hundreds of times faster than by hand, and the jet I fly allows me to be thousands of times more capable than I could be on my own. One way to illustrate this leverage is through the energy we use. The average person, despite physically generating only one hundred watts of electricity—about what a light bulb uses—now consumes over twelve thousand watts of energy. That energy powers the technology that amplifies our decisions. Today, the difference in outcome between a good decision and a bad decision has never been so great.

But what does it take to develop judgment and consistently make good decisions? Although decision-making is one of the most fundamental skills to master, it's not taught in most schools. Classes instead focus on convergent thinking whereby each problem has a single, well-defined solution. It's a method that was born out of the Industrial Revolution that's an efficient way for students to memorize facts as well as an easy way for teachers to assess the students. It's ill-suited, though, for the real world, which is messy and full of uncertainty and risk. However, just a little training can go a long way toward substantially improving a person's decision-making ability.

As fighter pilots, we've poured tremendous resources into finding ways to optimize a human's ability to make decisions. The training alone to develop an experienced fighter pilot costs nearly $50 million and takes almost a decade. I've been fortunate enough to have gone through the training twice— once to fly the F-16 and then again when I was selected to fly the F-35. I then served as an instructor, where I've taught hundreds of fighter pilots over the years. In my last active-duty assignment, I was the Chief of F-35 Training Systems, where I helped develop the next generation of fighter pilot training that will continue to serve as the bedrock of our air combat force over the next decade.

This book is a distillation of those lessons and how modern U.S. fighter pilots think about decision-making. Being on the cutting edge of applied decision-making, we've taught the techniques in this book to pilots around the world, including the Dutch, Danish, Israeli, Norwegian, South Korean, Japanese, and over a dozen other air forces. We've also had many other elite teams come and observe our training so they could incorporate our lessons into their own fields. We've taught surgeons, Super Bowl–winning coaches, CIA agents, Fortune 500 CEOs, NASA astronauts, and many

others who now successfully use these principles in their own ·
fields.

Storytelling is the most powerful way of imparting
knowledge. Outside of experiencing a lesson on your own,
stories allow for context, which, combined with knowledge,
produce understanding. With that in mind, I've drawn on
many stories—some from my own time flying fighter aircraft,
some from the business world, and some from key decisions
throughout history to help illustrate the different aspects of
the decision-making process and how they can be applied.

Knowledge is only useful to the degree that it can be drawn
on when it's needed. It doesn't matter how well information
can be recalled in a sterile environment—what matters is being able to use it in the real world, where there are distractions, uncertainty, and risk. Simplicity and usability must be
designed into any lesson from the beginning—it can't just
be an afterthought. Therefore, I've organized the book into
three sections—Assess, Choose, and Execute. These sections
form the pillars for how we make decisions as fighter pilots
through a concept known as the **ACE Helix**.

The first step is to **Assess** the problem. Without a proper
assessment of the problem, it's impossible to consistently
make good decisions. Many people, unfortunately, skip this
step; however, it's the foundation of good decision-making.
During the assess section, we'll look at a methodical way to
break down problems and to identify the most important
aspects by using concepts such as tipping points and power
laws.

We'll then transition into how to **Choose** the correct

course of action. In this section, we'll see how the decisions we've successfully encountered before form an interwoven web that makes up our instincts. For problems that we've never seen before, however, we'll look at tools that we can use to quickly assess the value of the different options we have available. We'll then see how a concept called *fast-forecasting* can enable us to quickly build a mental model where we can then extrapolate based off our existing instincts. We'll also explore the role of creativity in the decision-making process and how both people and organizations can develop more creative solutions, often unlocking exponential gains in value.

Finally, we'll focus on how to **Execute**. We'll discuss how to prioritize the tasks that arise from the decisions we make and how we can free up additional mental bandwidth to focus on the next decision that we inevitably need to make. We'll then look at the mind through a human-performance lens and see how, despite it being the single greatest tool in the world at making decisions, it can be fragile, prone to biases, and easily disrupted by emotions. We'll look at how we can have a greater degree of control over these factors and how, if we're unable to get to a neutral state, we can account for them during the decision-making process.

The reason a helix is used is because decisions are dynamic, often causing second- and third-order effects, which means they rarely end at the same point they started. A decision framework, therefore, needs to adapt as the conditions change. When graphed over time, this forms a helix. The shape also relates to how we fight. When dogfighting, most aircraft end up spiraling toward each other as each pilot makes decisions to put themselves in the best possible position to defeat the adversary. When looked at from the side, this often looks like a double helix—like a DNA structure.

THE WHY

Before I became a fighter pilot and learned these techniques, I struggled to consistently make good decisions. Often, I would make several good decisions in a row and then, seemingly out of nowhere, make a poor one. I wasn't intentional in how I made decisions, and I didn't have a framework for understanding them. With thousands of decisions to make each flight and a typical career lasting over a thousand flights, I realized it was important that I learn these techniques to the point that they were second nature. Today, although I still make mistakes every time I fly and have yet to fly a perfect mission—also known as a sortie—the difference between my good decisions and bad decisions is far narrower. The result is that I'm a much more effective fighter pilot than when I first started my career. The same is true for the decisions I make outside of the cockpit in everyday life—by utilizing the concepts in this book, I've developed to the point where most decisions are simple. I can quickly prioritize and then assess, choose, and execute on a decision before moving on to the next one.

When it comes to understanding ourselves and the world around us, it's often difficult to realize how much of an impact the accumulation of our decisions can make. Our decisions form the contact we make with the outside world—our relationships, our work, our health, our finances are all directly tied to the decisions we make. All of us deal with the consequences of our decisions; however, many rarely pause to think about how they arrived at them and how they can improve going forward. If most people did, I think the world would change—businesses would be more willing to innovate, people would be more critical of the content they consumed, there would be more financial security, people would be more willing to take calculated risks, and on and on.

There are a lot of books that are primarily focused on the academic theory behind decision-making. This book isn't one of them. More than anything else, it's meant to be actionable while also being entertaining—using storytelling so that the lessons can be remembered in a year, or five years, or a decade. My hope is that by the end of this book, you'll deliberately map out how you're making decisions. It may be different from what's in this book, which is fine—how we make decisions is predicated on our strengths and weaknesses and often varies depending on the field we're in and the problems we're solving. The most important part is being deliberate in making decisions and then debriefing afterward on how to improve. It's this iteration that over the last fifty years has developed United States fighter pilots into the most capable air force in the world—one that hasn't lost a U.S. soldier to enemy aircraft since April 15, 1953, and hasn't lost in an air-to-air engagement in over fifty years. Now it's your turn.

ASSESS

On May 31, 2009, Air France Flight 447 took off from Galeão International Airport in Rio de Janeiro, Brazil, bound for Charles de Gaulle Airport in Paris, France. The aircraft met its scheduled departure time of 7:30 p.m. and began climbing into the night sky. On board the aircraft were 216 passengers—208 adults, 8 children, and 1 infant. Supporting the flight were 9 flight attendants and 3 pilots with a combined flight time of over twenty thousand hours.

The aircraft was an Airbus A330, a twin-engine airliner that's still one of the most advanced aircraft flying today. Its digital fly-by-wire system and flight computers enable a sophisticated flight limit protection system that prevents it from stalling or exceeding structural limits. In the cockpit the traditional steering yoke and mechanical gauges have been replaced with a sleek side stick and six large screens to display information to the pilots. Although the aircraft was designed to be flown by two pilots, Flight 447 carried three so that each pilot could spend time resting during the scheduled eleven-hour flight across the ocean.

As the aircraft climbed and eventually leveled out, everything appeared to be uneventful. For the next several hours, it continued to fly along the Brazilian coastline, which eventually turned into the Atlantic Ocean. As it crossed the equator, the plane entered the intertropical convergence zone, an area where air from the Southern and Northern Hemispheres converge, typically forming a wall of thunderstorms. This night was no different—thunderstorms were reported in the area, but the routine weather hadn't affected a dozen other flights that had already shared similar routes to Flight 447.

As the aircraft continued over the Atlantic, the Brazilian controllers eventually lost contact with the flight, a not-uncommon occurrence as airliners cross the ocean. However, the next control center, located along the African coast, was never able to reach them. But, because a modern airliner vanishing was so far-fetched, they gave the aircraft a "virtual flight plan," which simulated the predicted flight path of the aircraft. For the next several hours, the simulated aircraft flew along its prescribed route, as it was programmed to do. It wasn't until the next morning that concern about the aircraft's whereabouts grew to the point where Air France finally alerted the authorities and an aerial search was launched from both sides of the Atlantic.

It took less than a day for patrol aircraft to find the wreckage of the aircraft five hundred miles off the coast of Brazil. Within the next week, over one thousand personnel were mobilized for the search, including dozens of aircraft and ships. One hundred thousand square miles of ocean were searched, but only bodies and debris were found. It was clear that all on board had been lost, but the question was *why*.

The answer was likely in the cockpit voice recorder and the flight data recorder, also known as the black boxes, that now lay on the ocean floor. The problem was that the area where Flight 447 had crashed was under *ten thousand* feet of water. To further complicate matters, the terrain was rugged: As one expert said, "It's a mountain range as big as the Alps. There was always the possibility that the wreckage from the aircraft disappeared down a crevasse. This is not a flat-bottom environment."

Initially, a specialized ship outfitted with miniature submarines was dispatched to find the wreckage. Time was of the essence—each black box was equipped with an underwater beacon that had only a thirty-day battery life, and once they stopped transmitting, the chances of finding them diminished dramatically. The United States Navy helped by lending towed pinger hydrophones. Even a French nuclear submarine joined the search.

However, by the end of July, nearly two months had passed, bringing to a close any hope of finding the black boxes through their beacons. The search then transitioned into the next phase, using towed sonar arrays to map the ocean floor to hopefully find the wreckage along with the critical black boxes. Back in Europe, a task force was set up to understand what brought the aircraft down. So far, they had only concluded that:

1. There was poor weather along the airplane's planned route of flight.

2. The aircraft's onboard systems had sent several automated messages broadcasting that there was a disagreement in the airspeed readings during the final minutes of the flight.

3. Based on debris found, the aircraft didn't break up in flight but rather struck the ocean in an odd way—it had a normal flight attitude but with a high rate of descent, almost as if it had been dropped on its belly.

These facts ruled out early theories such as a bomb exploding or extreme turbulence ripping off the wings. More than likely, poor weather had caused icing on the plane's pitot tubes—devices that measure the speed of the aircraft—which then triggered the automated broadcasts about inconsistent airspeeds. This in and of itself wasn't enough to bring down a plane. In fact, there had been fifteen similar incidents in *just the previous year* throughout Air France's Airbus A330 fleet. In each of the cases, the pilots had no trouble flying through the conditions. Indicated airspeed has no bearing on how an aircraft flies—similar to a broken speedometer in a car, the pilots could just disregard it until the ice melted and it started working again. In the case of Air France Flight 447, the investigators theorized, the icing must have set off a catastrophic chain of events that eventually ended with the crew losing control of the aircraft. Over the next two years, that was as far as the investigators could come to re-creating the crash without the black boxes. Changes were made to prevent the pitot tubes from icing over and the handoff between air traffic control centers was updated to prevent a similar delay if another aircraft went missing. However, it wasn't until April 2011, when the recovery was on its fourth search attempt, that the wreckage was finally found. Using autonomous underwater vehicles equipped with side-scan sonars, a debris field was found in a silty area of the ocean floor over thirteen thousand feet beneath the surface.

Within a month, the black boxes were found and raised from the ocean floor. They were then, under judicial seal, taken by the French Navy to the port of Cayenne and then quickly flown to Paris to be downloaded and analyzed. What the investigators found shocked the aviation world and would go on to provide a master class to generations of pilots on decision-making.

STAND-UPS

Throughout U.S. Air Force pilot training, students have what are called *stand-ups* each morning. All the students sit along the walls of a classroom while an instructor stands at the front. A student is randomly selected to stand in the middle of the classroom, and a theoretical emergency is then given to the student. The atmosphere is intentionally tense to replicate some of the fear and adrenaline that can be felt when a pilot encounters an emergency in the air. If the student handles the emergency poorly, they're told to sit down and another student takes over for them. The performance is closely documented and factors into the type of aircraft they receive at the end of pilot training. To further increase the pressure, the entire class can be punished if a student does poorly enough.

As you can imagine, students don't enjoy stand-ups—I

know I didn't when I went through. When my name was called, I'd take a deep breath, mentally lock in, and walk to the middle of the classroom. I'd then say the phrase we all had to repeat before starting, which was, "I will maintain aircraft control, analyze the situation, take proper action, and land as soon as conditions permit." I would then talk through every switch actuation and radio call as if I were actually flying the aircraft.

What we were learning was a framework for making decisions that had been developed over nearly a century of flight, where one poor decision can result in the loss of life. Though it wasn't enjoyable, it provided deliberate practice at solving complex problems under pressure.

Unlike most of my tests in school, there wasn't just one solution to each problem. Stand-ups required divergent thinking, whereby each decision had multiple correct answers and relied on the students to understand the cascading second- and third-order consequences. A rash, seemingly simple decision early on could lead to an unsolvable problem fifteen minutes later. For many students—even those who had graduated at the top of their class while in college or at the Air Force Academy—this proved to be exceptionally difficult. Their minds had been honed in the academic world, and they struggled to quickly come up with solutions to unpredictable problems.

I remember one student who had meticulously written down every conceivable problem that he could think of along with their solutions, filling several notebooks in the process. Early in the course, when the problems were simple, he was able to reference his notebooks and quickly solve the emergency. However, midway through the training, when the problems became more complex and often included multiple emergencies at the same time, his method became a hinderance. It lacked flexibility and when he encountered problems that diverged from what he was expecting, he couldn't adapt and crumbled under the pressure. Eventually, it spiraled to the point where he could no longer safely handle an emergency and was washed out of the training.

Before we'd even started stand-ups, though, the instructors had already given us the keys to success. In fact, it could be found in the initial phrase that we had to repeat each time our name was called: "I will maintain aircraft control and then analyze the situation." *Maintain aircraft control* meant that even during an emergency, we still needed to fly the plane. Being in a single-seat aircraft, you don't have the luxury of disconnecting and focusing all your attention on the problem at hand. You need to split your mental resources between the malfunction and the flying of the aircraft.

Next was analyzing the situation. Developing a proper understanding of the problem is the first step to solving it. Our instinct is often to bypass this critical step and begin acting. It's a cognitive bias for many people and organizations, whereby we believe that the sooner we start fixing a problem, the sooner we'll solve it. It's such a strong instinct that when learning to fly the F-16, there's an unorthodox technique taught to new pilots to prevent them from skipping this important step.

In the cockpit of the F-16, there's a tiny analog clock built into the lower right-hand corner of the console that's a holdover from when it was designed in the 1970s. Nearly everything else in the jet has been upgraded and replaced over the years, but the tiny hand-wound clock remains. Though no one uses it to keep time, seasoned instructors would say, "Before you make a decision, wind the clock." It was a seemingly useless process; however, it prevented people's first inclination of rushing to solve the problem. Winding the clock occupied the pilot's attention for just a few seconds and physically prevented them from touching anything else. It forced their brain to spend time assessing the situation *before* they acted, allowing them to make far better decisions.

THE FINAL MINUTES

Inside Air France Flight 447's black boxes, the recordings showed that the first several hours of the flight were quiet. The captain, Marc Dubois, along with the second copilot, Pierre-Cédric Bonin, attended to routine flight operations while having time to talk about their personal lives. At fifty-eight years old, Dubois was highly experienced with almost eleven thousand flight hours, nearly half of those as a captain in command of the aircraft. In the cockpit voice recordings, his demeanor stands out—he's calm and thoughtful, serving as a mentor to the crew while also coaching them on how he's making his decisions.

His copilot Bonin, however, is inexperienced and, at thirty-two years old, is known as the "company baby." Bonin is traveling with his wife, who is a passenger on board the aircraft. Prior to the trip, the two had dropped their two kids off at their grandparents' house so that they could take advantage of the long holiday weekend. In the voice recordings, Bonin's inexperience comes through, as he appears jumpy and un-sure of his decisions, even during routine tasks.

Also on board the aircraft is another copilot, David Rob-ert, who spent the first several hours sleeping in the pilot rest compartment located just behind the cockpit. He's another seasoned pilot with over 6,500 flight hours and is a graduate of the Ecole Nationale de l'Aviation Civile, the most presti-gious aviation school in France. Although Robert is highly experienced, he recently transitioned to a management job at the airline's operations center and only flew occasionally to maintain his status as a pilot.

After three and a half hours of routine operations, the air-craft encountered the outskirts of the storms along the in-tertropical convergence zone and began passing through the upper-layer clouds. Normally, the crew would have climbed above the weather; however, because the outside air tempera-ture was higher than normal and the aircraft was still heavily loaded with fuel for the transatlantic flight, they could only climb to thirty-five thousand feet, forcing them through the weather instead of over it. The turbulence began increasing and a phenomenon known as Saint Elmo's fire began occur-ring, whereby the electric charge of the storm caused blue and violet fluorescent flashes across the cockpit windows. Bonin had never seen it before, and in the recording, he seems both fascinated and worried by its presence. He points out that the aircraft could climb slightly higher if they wanted to, a sub-tle request to the captain. Dubois, however, has seen similar conditions hundreds of times before. Unfazed, he continues the flightpath while ringing his replacement so that he can take his scheduled sleep break. Copilot Robert then enters the cockpit and swaps places with the captain. Strangely, despite Robert being far more experienced than Bonin with over twice his flight hours, the captain leaves Bonin in charge of the aircraft.

After the captain leaves, Robert and Bonin begin discussing the weather. Unlike other aircraft in the area, they hadn't requested a deviation around the storm cells. Looking at the aircraft's weather radar, they realize that they're about to pass through a cell, and ring back to the flight attendants.

> BONIN: Listen, in two minutes, we're going to be getting into an area where things are going to be moving around a little bit more than now. You'll want to take care.
> FLIGHT ATTENDANT: Okay, we should sit down, then?
> BONIN: Well, I think that's not a bad idea . . .

Bonin's inexperience is evident—he's seen the weather radar and has the most situational awareness about the storm. The flight attendant is asking for direction, but Bonin appears to still be in a junior copilot mindset, deferring his decisions despite now being the pilot in command of the aircraft.

The two copilots then discuss the unusually elevated outside temperature preventing them from climbing to their desired altitude. Bonin is happy they're flying an Airbus A330, saying, "Bloody hell, thank God we're in an A330, eh?" To which Robert coolly replies, "Dead right."

As they continue to fly through the clouds, Bonin becomes worried about ice building up on the wings and says, "Let's go for the anti-icing system, it's better than nothing."

Following up with, "We seem to be at the end of the cloud layer. It might be okay."

Look at those last three statements by Bonin; they're all an attempt to reason with himself that everything is going to be okay. Also in the recording, it's clear that Bonin's voice has a higher pitch than before, and he's talking faster. If we were able to measure his heart rate and respiration, they would likely be elevated. He's afraid. I've been there—you can feel the weight of responsibility on your shoulders and you're not quite sure what to do. You try to calm yourself down by saying things like, "It might be okay." At the same time, you look for reassurance by saying things like, "Thank God we're in an A330, right?" Bonin's wife is also aboard the plane, likely adding to his stress.

Soon thereafter, Robert realizes that the radar system has not been set to the correct mode. Changing the settings, he realizes that they're now headed directly toward an area of intense activity.

ROBERT: You can possibly pull a little to the left.
BONIN: Sorry, what?
ROBERT: You can possibly pull it a little to the left. We're agreed that we're in manual, yeah?

Bonin begins banking the plane to the left when, suddenly, a strange aroma of charged electricity floods the cockpit along with an increase in temperature.

BONIN: Holy cow, did you touch the air-conditioning?
ROBERT: I didn't touch it.
BONIN: What's that smell?

Robert, who's flown similar trips, recognizes the smell as ozone, a by-product from the electrically charged storms they're flying through.

BONIN: Is this ozone? Are we sure?
ROBERT: This is the reason for—
BONIN: Well, I can feel that it's already incredibly hotter!
ROBERT: It's this, that is hot and ozone-y. [Presumably pointing to the thunderstorm cells appearing on their weather radar.]

The aircraft then begins encountering hail—it's the humid tropical air being sucked up from the ocean and rapidly freezing at high altitude. In the recording, you can hear a crackling white noise, like fingernails tapping on metal, as the tiny ice grains collide with the aircraft. Bonin is clearly even more uncomfortable now—although he's the pilot in command, he keeps deferring to Robert for what they should do.

To minimize the structural strain on the aircraft, the copilots reduce their speed, and then to protect the engines from icing, they turn on the engine anti-ice system. Although the hail is small enough that it doesn't pose a threat to the structure of the aircraft, its small size allows it to begin accumulating on the inside of the pitot tubes.

An aircraft's pitot tubes are responsible for measuring the speed of the aircraft. The tiny probes sit at the front of the aircraft and measure the pressure of the wind against them. That pressure is then translated into an airspeed that's shown to the pilots as well as fed into the aircraft's advanced flight control computers. For redundancy, the Airbus A330 has three pitot tubes. Unfortunately, for Flight 447, all three became blocked nearly simultaneously.

Without a valid airspeed to control the plane, the autopilot became confused and disconnected, immediately handing full control of the aircraft over to the pilots. It's important to note, though, that the aircraft hadn't suffered any mechanical malfunction—it was level at thirty-five thousand feet, and aside from the loss of airspeed indication, was continuing to fly as designed. If Bonin and Robert had done nothing, the plane would have continued flying straight ahead. Within a few minutes, the pitot tube heating would have melted the blockages, and the trip would have continued on as planned.

In the recordings, as soon as the autopilot disconnects, an alarm sounds along with a flashing master warning light indicating that the plane is now under manual control. Bonin then says, "I have the controls," reaffirming that he is in charge and flying and that Robert is the copilot who will assist him.

ASSESS THE PROBLEM

This is the moment of truth. The plane is in near-perfect working order, while Bonin is now trying to understand why the autopilot has just disconnected. If he was afraid in the minutes leading up to the autopilot disconnecting, he's now likely terrified. The proper thing to do here is what's called a *cross-check,* whereby he compares the airspeed indicator with the other instrument readings in the cockpit, such as ground speed, altitude, attitude, and rate of climb. This would have allowed him to realize that only his airspeed indicator wasn't working, enabling him to temporarily disregard it while flying off the other instruments.

Bonin, however, acts. He doesn't assess the situation and immediately pulls back on the stick, putting the aircraft into a steep climb. It's an irrational decision, as just minutes earlier, he was discussing the fact that the plane couldn't climb any higher due to the high external temperature. However, as stress increases, our IQ level decreases, and we often make poor decisions. Bonin has now made the situation significantly worse.

A warning chime begins going off, alerting the pilots that the aircraft has left the programmed altitude. As Bonin continues to pull back on the stick, the aircraft begins a blistering climb of seven thousand feet per minute. In the thin air at high altitude, it's unsustainable. The aircraft begins rapidly losing airspeed.

BONIN: There's no good . . . there's no good speed indication.
ROBERT: We've lost the speeds, then? Pay attention to your speed. Watch your speed.
BONIN: Okay, okay, I'm descending.

Robert is in a difficult position. He's experienced, but rusty now that he only flies occasionally. This is one of the most dangerous situations for a pilot—your confidence often doesn't match your ability. He's also at the bottom of his circadian rhythm and likely tired. Most importantly, despite being vastly more experienced, he's been relegated to a backup role. Exacerbating the situation, the Airbus's flight controls, unlike older aircraft, weren't designed to show the pilot what the other pilot was doing with their side stick.

> ROBERT: Descend . . . It says we're going up . . . It says we're going up, so descend.
> BONIN: Okay.
> ROBERT: You're at . . . Go back down!
> BONIN: We're in . . . Yeah, we're in a climb.

Robert understands the situation: The aircraft's in a steep climb, and the biggest threat is stalling, whereby the aircraft's speed decreases to the point where it can't generate enough lift and begins falling. This wasn't even something that was supposed to be possible on the Airbus A330. The engineers had designed it so that the pilots couldn't put the aircraft in a dangerous situation. The company had advertised their system by saying: "Fly-By-Wire offers improved handling, commonality across the Airbus family, and a flight envelope protection system so that pilots can push aircraft to their limits, without ever extending them."

Unfortunately for Flight 447, once the flight computers recognized they were getting erroneous data from the pitot tubes, the system transitioned into a backup mode, whereby it shut off the flight envelope protection system.

Less than a minute later, with the airspeed rapidly decreasing, the aircraft stalls. An alarm goes off along with master warning lights and a synthesized voice saying, "Stall, stall!"

Due to the turbulent airflow over the wings, the plane begins buffeting. Understanding the urgency of the situation, Robert rings for the captain to immediately come back to the cockpit.

Though Flight 447 has stalled, they are still in an easily recoverable situation. With thirty-eight thousand feet of altitude, they have ample time to simply push forward on the stick, regain airspeed, and continue flying. Until the stall, Robert seemed to be narrowing in on the problem; however, because of the side stick—instead of a connected yoke like older airliners—he doesn't know that Bonin has been holding the stick back the entire time. He suspects icing of the wings and activates the wing deicing system.

During the confusion, one of the pitot tubes begins working again, giving conflicting information as to the actual airspeed of the aircraft. Robert then spends time adjusting the avionics to a standby setting to hopefully isolate the problem and regain an accurate picture of the plane's condition. This, however, makes the situation worse, since the standby pitot tube is still blocked. After spending time focused on manipulating the avionics, Robert begins losing situational awareness. Once he finishes and returns his attention to flying the aircraft, he's now just as confused as Bonin. At this point, the plane is now falling at more than a mile a minute.

ROBERT: We still have the engine! What the hell is happening? I don't understand what's happening. Do you understand what's happening or not?

BONIN: Damn it, I don't have control of the plane. I don't have control of the plane at all!

ROBERT: Left seat taking control!

Robert takes over and begins to counter the roll; however, he too seems to be unaware of the fact that the plane is stalled and pulls slightly back on the stick. Bonin, however, without warning, violates a basic rule of airmanship and begins pulling back on his stick with maximum force, continuing to stall the aircraft and further confusing Robert.

By now, the plane is falling at over ten thousand feet a minute, but because Bonin was still pulling back on the stick, the nose is pointing up as though it were climbing, similar to a leaf falling from a tree. With the anti-ice system activated, the pitot tubes quickly melt the ice and become fully functional, showing an accurate forward airspeed of less than seventy miles per hour. This was a situation that the engineers had never accounted for. The onboard flight computers are now just as confused as the pilots and, suspecting a fault in the code, turn off the stall warning, signaling to the pilots that the situation is improving.

A minute and a half after the crisis began, Captain Dubois returns to the cockpit, likely having just woken up.

DUBOIS: What the hell are you doing?
BONIN: We've lost control of the plane!
ROBERT: We've totally lost control of the plane . . . We don't understand anything . . . We've tried everything! What should we do?
DUBOIS: Well, I don't know.

The captain is in an even tougher situation than Robert. Just minutes before, he was likely sleeping when the aircraft started buffeting and then stalled. He then gets a call from the copilots and quickly makes his way into the cockpit. There he finds the instrument console illuminated with master caution and warning lights along with his two copilots shouting at him that the aircraft is out of control. Due to the intense gyrations, he elects to not swap out with one of the copilots and decides to sit in the jump seat behind them to try to troubleshoot the situation.

Bonin then moves the engine levers to idle, the opposite of what's needed. As the thrust decreases, the nose sinks into a dive. The aircraft is now falling at an extreme thirteen thousand feet per minute. He then deploys the air brakes, further exacerbating the situation.

> BONIN: I have the impression that we are flying at an incredibly high speed, right? What do you think?
> ROBERT: No, above all, don't extend them!

Robert pushes the engine levers fully forward, and the engines begin producing maximum thrust. The pilots then discuss the situation and why the aircraft is out of control. Bonin appears the most confused, asking at one point whether they are really going down. Throughout this, the aircraft is continuing to fall and is now only ten thousand feet above the ocean. In desperation, Robert begins speaking directly to the aircraft, saying, "Climb, climb, climb, climb." Hearing this, Bonin says, "But I've been at maximum nose-up for a while."

For a moment, there's silence in the cockpit. *This* is the critical piece of information that Robert and Captain Dubois have been missing.

Until this point, they had no idea that Bonin had been holding back on the stick the whole time and therefore stalling the aircraft.

DUBOIS: No, no, no! Don't go up! No, no, no!
ROBERT: Go down!

Robert then pushes his stick forward, attempting to break the stall. Bonin, however, is still pulling back on his stick. The aircraft recognizes this and activates a warning, letting the pilots know that they're both trying to control the plane.

ROBERT: Give me the controls—the controls to me!
BONIN: Go ahead, you have the controls . . .

Finally, the aircraft pitches down, and its airspeed begins to increase. They are now only five thousand feet above the ocean—it's still possible to recover the aircraft but the margin of error is quickly shrinking. Bonin, however, is still panicking, and within ten seconds, he begins pulling back on the stick again.

At two thousand feet, the aircraft's ground proximity warning system triggers, activating a synthetic voice that says, "Pull up! Pull up!" With no hope for a recovery, the captain then tells them to pull up to hopefully reduce the force of the impact.

DUBOIS: Go on, pull up.
BONIN: We're going to crash! This can't be true! But what's happening?

ROBERT: We are dead.

DUBOIS: Ten degrees of pitch . . .

One-point-four seconds later, the aircraft slammed into the water, belly first, at 123 miles per hour. The collision, at more than 51 times the force of gravity, broke apart the plane before it quickly sank into the ocean. All 228 passengers and crew died on impact from the extreme trauma. From beginning to end, the entire event lasted less than five minutes.

ANALYSIS

I've analyzed the crash and listened to the cockpit recording more times than I care to count, and every time, I'm surprised at how chilling those last words are. How did a routine flight go so wrong so fast?

There are dozens of contributing factors for why the aircraft went down; however, the root cause is that none of the pilots had a correct mental model of what was happening until it was too late. Bonin forgot—or never learned—the very first step to making a decision: **Assess** the problem.

Bonin was clearly scared in the moments leading up to the autopilot disconnecting and likely terrified after. He skipped assessing the problem and immediately acted by pulling fully back on the stick, a reckless action for a plane full of passengers traveling at thirty-five thousand feet in the thin atmosphere. A modern airliner is relatively easy to fly—the engineers designed it to default to flying straight and level. By pulling back on the stick, Bonin made the situation unstable, and it was only a matter of time before the plane stalled.

Robert, the more experienced copilot, never had the luxury of analyzing a stable aircraft. Instead, he was thrust into a dynamic situation. Despite this disadvantage, he was still agonizingly close to understanding the problem during several points throughout the stall. However, every time he made progress, Bonin would try something different, further clouding his understanding of what was happening.

In retrospect, the captain shouldn't have handed off the aircraft to an inexperienced copilot before entering the storm. Once he did, he gave up his situational awareness and became a passenger. Moments before the autopilot disconnected, he was in the pilot rest compartment, likely sleeping. Groggy and rushing back to the cockpit, he encountered a chaotic scene with the airliner dropping at over thirteen thousand feet per minute and two copilots panicking. Captain Dubois never had a chance to build an accurate mental model of the situation until the final seconds, when Bonin told him that he had been holding the stick back the entire time. By then, it was too late.

Aviation is a high-wire act where the outcome of a single poor decision can often be catastrophic. It's a profession where you always have skin in the game. As the saying goes, old bad pilots don't exist because mistakes often end in fatalities. That's why there's such a strong focus on decision-making, always through the lens of "Is it actionable?" Academic theory is not sufficient—the training is only useful if it can be applied in the real world.

When I hear that a pilot has crashed—even if it's entirely pilot error—my first thought is empathy for the pilot and their family, while an old quote comes to mind:

> Whenever we talk about a pilot who has been killed in a flying accident, we should all keep one thing in mind. He called upon the sum of all his knowledge and made a judgment. He believed in it so strongly that he knowingly bet his life on it. That his judgment was faulty is tragic . . . Every instructor, supervisor, and contemporary who ever spoke to him had an opportunity to influence his judgment, so a little bit of all of us goes with every pilot we lose.
>
> —ANONYMOUS

The decisions we make form the connections we have with the world around us. It's only by first assessing the problem that we can gain enough understanding to reliably make the right decision. When flying fighters, we'll use a cross-check to build our assessment. All our senses contribute to the model. What are the instruments displaying? What's going on outside of the aircraft? What sort of vibrations can be felt? How are the g-forces changing? What radio calls or alarms can you hear? Is there a smell of smoke or fumes? Buried within all the data is the information that's needed to solve the problem at hand.

Instead of trying to multitask—something humans are notoriously bad at—we'll spend anywhere from a fraction of a second to several seconds understanding each piece of information before moving on to the next one. The key is to not let yourself focus on just one data source at the expense of the rest—something we call *getting sucked into the soda straw*. When that happens, the pilot will quickly lose sight of the big picture and be unable to see how their actions fit the larger system they're operating within.

The ability to make sense of a chaotic environment while simplifying and structuring information is not just applicable to flying, it's a fundamental skill that's required to navigate our increasingly complex world. We're saturated with hundreds of times more information than previous generations. What's required is a way to quickly sift through the noise to understand key parts of a system so that we can then create an outsize impact given our time and resources. This requires judgment, and judgment requires nonlinear thinking.

POWER LAWS

As I merged at over one thousand miles per hour against the F-16 I was fighting, I could, for a split second, see the other pilot at the controls as he rapidly passed me in the opposite direction, his green flight suit blending into his metallic visor as he tracked my aircraft. In my F-16, I started a hard turn back toward him while pushing the throttle fully forward into maximum afterburner.

This was one of my first fighter training missions in the sky above the Arizona desert. After finishing undergraduate pilot training, I was now flying my top choice, the legendary F-16 Fighting Falcon, known by fighter pilots as simply the Viper. After months of academics and simulators, we were now in the beginning stages of learning how to transition from being pilots to being fighter pilots. That meant learning how to max-perform the aircraft while balancing risk and reward against a thinking adversary. If we were overly cautious, the enemy would use the excess margin of safety against us in their tactics; however, if we accepted too much risk, we could put ourselves and others into an unnecessarily dangerous position. It was a fine line that we as new fighter pilots were learning to navigate.

For the sortie today, I was fighting one of the most experienced instructor pilots on the base—a full-bird colonel who oversaw the entire reserve wing, consisting of over two thousand personnel. He had multiple combat deployments, and during the early days of the Iraq War, he had prevented a group of U.S. soldiers from being overrun by the enemy. He was the pilot that we, brand-new lieutenants, all aspired to be like.

As our aircraft passed each other, I rolled inverted and pulled back on the stick. The giant control surfaces of my F-16 dug into the airstream as the g-forces rapidly increased. On the ground, I weigh 200 pounds, 230 with my gear on. If you've ever been in a roller coaster that's done a loop where your head felt like it was being pushed down, that's about three g's. Within a second, I was now under nine times the force of gravity with over two thousand pounds of force crushing me into my seat.

Blood was now being pulled from my brain into my arms and legs; if I lost enough, I would black out and lose consciousness, a term we refer to as a *G-LOC* (g-force induced loss of consciousness). Pointed straight down at over seven hundred miles per hour, I would likely impact the ground before I woke up, which unfortunately has been responsible for many fighter pilot deaths over the years.

To counter the effects, I started my anti-G straining maneuver—a special set of muscle contractions and breathing to push the blood back into my brain. I was also wearing a

G suit, which are pants that are fitted with air bladders that squeeze the legs and prevent blood from rushing into them. Even with my gear and training, though, I could still feel the effects as the blood drained out of my head and my peripheral vision shrank until it looked as though I were seeing the world through a paper towel roll.

My body and limbs were now pinned into my seat—even if I wanted to reach up, it would be impossible with each arm now weighing over 250 pounds. I could feel the enormous pressure in my chest—like a car being parked on it—as my mask injected pressurized air into my lungs to augment my breathing.

As I maintained sight of the adversary over my shoulder with my helmet wedged between the canopy and the seat, I could see that he too had rolled inverted—we were now less than a mile apart, both pointed straight down as we continued turning back toward each other.

Through my helmet's augmented reality display, I could see a diamond following him—the symbol for an enemy—along with all the necessary information I needed to fight him. As we began pointing at each other again, I tried to shoot a missile at him while also defending my aircraft by deploying flares to mask my heat signature. Within seconds, though, we were both inside the minimum range for our missiles as we continued toward a second merge—the fight would now likely be decided by the gun.

We passed each other again—this time so close that I could see the writing on the side of his jet. He was changing tactics. Instead of continuing to spiral down, he rotated his wings and began pulling straight up into the vertical. I could see a large vapor cloud now leaping off the back of his jet as the low pressure from the extreme maneuver caused the air to rapidly condense and form a cloud behind him. To win, I would have to match him by pulling straight up into the air—only I was too slow for the maneuver, by five knots, or just six miles per hour.

While trying to keep sight of the adversary under high g-forces, I had let my airspeed drop out of my cross-check. Based on the feel of the jet, I knew I was cutting it close but decided to still match the aggressive strategy. I assumed—incorrectly—that being slightly slow would only have a small effect on the outcome of the maneuver. I set my wings and pulled straight up while pushing even harder on the throttle with the hopes that the jet would give me extra thrust. I was now committed to matching him as we both rocketed skyward.

As I continued toward the top of the loop, my airspeed rapidly decreased. In the cockpit, a warning horn began letting me know that I was about to enter a dangerous flight condition. I tried to abort the maneuver and roll off to the horizon. The jet was too slow. I was now traveling slower than a car on a highway, and without wind resistance on the flight controls, I was no longer an aircraft, just thirty thousand pounds of metal arcing through the air.

The aircraft made it agonizingly close to the top of the loop, but right before it did, my airspeed went to zero. For a split second, I was balancing on the tail of my aircraft as the afterburner fought against gravity. If I had been at sea level, I would have had more thrust than weight, and I would have been able to accelerate out of the stall. However, at my current altitude, the thrust wasn't enough to overcome the pull of gravity, and I began slowly traveling backward—something the F-16 wasn't designed to do.

The F-16 has multiple flight computers to assess how it's flying. Immediately, it realized that it was outside of design limits and began alerting me with an audible "Caution, caution" and "Warning, warning" while illuminating the flight control system warning lights. The nose of the jet then snapped down at negative 2.4 g's. If you've been in a car that crested a hill, and you felt your stomach drop, that's about half a g—if I put you on a scale, you would weigh half of what you normally do. At negative 2.4 g's, I was now being pulled off my seat with over five hundred pounds of force. Everything that wasn't strapped down ricocheted throughout the cockpit. Even my body, which was connected to the seat through my harness, lifted off the seat several inches as it strained against the shoulder straps. The blood in my body now rushed upward, filling my head and eyes with excess blood and turning my vision a shade of red.

Looking at my altitude, I realized that I had already dropped five thousand feet as the nose of the jet sliced through the air in a figure-eight motion as it hunted for airflow. At that rate, there wasn't much time before I impacted the ground. I looked down between my legs to find the yellow-and-black ejection handle. Pulling it would cause the canopy to blow off while igniting a rocket motor in my seat that would quickly separate me from the aircraft. I wanted to make sure despite being lifted off the seat and being thrown around the cockpit that when the time came, I could still pull it. In the back of my mind, I was thinking about how things had gone so wrong so fast.

POWER LAWS

One of the sayings fighter pilots have is, "There's no problem so bad you can't make it worse." What that means is that the aircraft we fly are incredibly complex and often operating at the outer edges of the performance envelope. It's an unforgiving environment where even one wrong switch actuation can cause a catastrophic breakup. For instance, with a stabilizer fail warning, here's what the emergency checklist says:

- Speed brake use may cause loss of aircraft control.
- Loss of aircraft control may occur immediately at less than XXX knots.
- Frequent control stick inputs, even small amplitude, will result in increased heating and may cause loss of aircraft control.

All three of those actions are seemingly benign, but coupled with a stabilizer failure, they can cause the aircraft to quickly become uncontrollable and crash.

Fighter aircraft are inherently unstable systems where a tiny input at the wrong time or wrong point can cause the design limit to be exceeded, resulting in a crash or catastrophic breakup. Throughout the flight regime, there are hundreds of these less intuitive areas where a pilot can quickly get themselves into trouble. It's important, therefore, for a pilot to be able to quickly assess a situation and map out these key points so that they can incorporate them into their mental model. The edge of the performance envelope isn't smooth but rather a jagged edge that the pilot must learn to navigate. This skill, though, has broad-reaching applications far beyond the cockpit.

Many problems in life are nonlinear, whereby small changes can produce large outcomes. This often goes against our natural inclination. Decades of research in cognitive psychology show that our brains struggle to understand these types of relationships. They're biased toward linear thinking—if you walk thirty steps, you are now thirty steps away from where you started; to walk twice as far, it'll take twice as long. However, this thinking can often lead us astray. For example, imagine that you have two vehicles that are each driven ten thousand miles per year—a car that gets 20 MPG (miles per gallon) and a truck that gets 10 MPG. To reduce costs, which is a better upgrade?

a. Replacing the 10 MPG truck with a 20 MPG truck
b. Replacing the 20 MPG car with a 50 MPG car

When given this problem, most people choose the car—an increase of 30 MPG is both greater and a larger percentage increase when compared to the truck. However, the answer is, counterintuitively, that replacing the truck is a better value. The current truck uses one thousand gallons of gas per year, while the car uses five hundred gallons. Replacing the truck will reduce the amount of gas used by five hundred gallons while replacing the car will only reduce it by three hundred gallons.

If you're surprised, it's because your mind has reduced the relationship to a linear problem. However, as MPG increases, the total gas saved decreases at a smaller and smaller rate. The effect is so great that even if we replaced the car with an ultraefficient 100 MPG car, we would *still* save more by replacing the truck.

To emphasize the point of how our minds are biased toward linear thinking, let's look at another example: If I were to give you a penny and tell you that it would double in value each day for the next month, after thirty-one days, how much money would you have? Go ahead and stop and think about it.

Most people's guesses are on the order of several hundred dollars—nonlinear thinking doesn't come naturally to us. Even after hearing that this is an exponential problem, many people's guesses aren't usually more than a few hundred thousand dollars. The answer, in fact, is over $10 million.

To make things even more difficult, there are often points—called *knees in the curve*—where values begin to rapidly change. Take the penny example—if I told you that it would double each day for twenty days instead of thirty-one, what would your estimate be? With two-thirds of the time, a linear guess would be $6 million. But since this is a nonlinear problem, you might guess something significantly lower, like $500,000. The answer is just $20,000—less than *1 percent* of the total value after a full month. Day twenty is the knee in the curve where the value begins to rapidly change.

To understand the world we live in, we need to understand

these nonlinear relationships, which fall under the term *power laws*. Power laws govern systems where a change in one aspect can lead to a very large change in another, regardless of the starting conditions. While the definition may sound abstract, all of us have experience with power laws in our lives. When someone starts working out for the first time, they'll initially see rapid progress as their strength quickly increases. However, their gains will eventually begin to slow despite putting in the same amount of effort. Even with increased effort, their ability will eventually plateau. That's why there's such a narrow gap among Olympic athletes—everyone has optimized their bodies and techniques and are now fighting for fractional gains in performance.

Even though most people are familiar with power laws, few are adept at consistently bringing them into their decision-making. Because power laws can have such an outsize effect on outcomes, it's important to be able to quickly identify them and understand their implications. For a multitude of reasons, people consistently fail to account for them, which often leads to a skewed assessment of the problem they're facing and results in a poor decision. Let's look at a business example.

THE TRILLION-DOLLAR MISS

In the winter of 1997, several Stanford students arrived at a business meeting at a restaurant named Fuki Sushi in Palo Alto, California. By then, the modest restaurant had already become a staple of Silicon Valley, having been the first Japanese restaurant to open in the area twenty years earlier. Entering the door, the students were greeted by a bright neon SUSHI sign that stood in stark contrast to the traditionally dressed Japanese chefs preparing meals.

This meeting was unique because the students had with them a revolutionary algorithm they called BackRub. They had started on it several years earlier during a school project and were working on it part-time from their Stanford dorm rooms. By now, the students were, incredibly, using *over half* of Stanford's internet bandwidth. However, with no business model behind it, the students only saw the program as a stepping stone in their academic careers.

The algorithm was revolutionary because it had the ability to bring order to the internet in a scalable way. The internet, which began as a way for academic institutions to share research papers, had quickly devolved into the digital Wild West. By design, the internet was decentralized, which made it impossible to standardize. Anyone could upload their thoughts, images, products, and code in whatever format they wanted. It was an ever-expanding digital world on the brink of becoming overwhelmed with spam. The question that everyone was now asking was: How do you organize the vast quantity of information in a way that's useful?

The solution, it seemed, was web portals. Companies such as America Online, Excite, and Yahoo! curated the internet's content into elaborate home pages with everything that users needed. Unlike today, with artificial intelligence and machine learning to customize the user experience, these home screens were a one-size-fits-all solution. The web portals were, in effect, digital newspapers. Users would log on and browse through the curated content—clicking on the links that interested them. This was fine for most users—many of whom only had a few hours of experience on the internet. The problem was that this only gave them access to a fraction of the information available.

Many portals, though, did provide a tiny box at the bottom of their screens for specific searches. Before running a search, users had to select from a drop-down menu with several options: The default was to just search through the curated content on the portal, the second option was to search through preselected news sites, and the last option was to search the entire internet—something users did less than 5 percent of the time. The reason was, in addition to being a new concept, the results were *terrible*. Endless pages of spam would be returned to the user, who would be forced to manually sift through the results. After a few failed search attempts, the average user would write off the feature as a gimmick and never try it again.

EXCITE

Sitting across the table from the students at Fuki Sushi were two of the founders of the goliath tech company Excite.com. Excite was the second-largest web portal in the world and the fourth-most-visited website on the internet. Excite had recently gone public and was now valued at over $5 billion. Excite was unique, because unlike other portals, which were run as media companies, it had been started as a tech company focusing on the infrastructure behind the content. So far, the strategy had paid off, giving them a technological advantage over their competitors and making them one of the fastest-growing companies in the world. However, despite their growth and valuation, the founders knew that their company's long-term survival depended on cracking the search problem.

On the surface, the search problem looked simple—you used the keywords that users typed into a search box and matched them to how often they appeared on websites. The most similar results would be ranked highest. This wasn't a new concept—computers had been around for nearly thirty years by this point, and *information retrieval,* as it's called, was a commonly used technique. However, the technique only worked well in academic settings with a few thousand people uploading high-quality, standardized content. Because the internet was scaling exponentially and most of it was spam, information retrieval was now failing. This problem had led to a growing sentiment among experts that the internet wasn't tamable and therefore wouldn't be as revolutionary as they had hoped. As Barry Rubinson, the director of engineering at one of the leading search engines, said at the time, "It's all wizard and witchcraft. Anyone who tells you it's scientific is just pulling your leg. The first problem is that relevance is in the eye of the beholder. The second is making sense of the infuriatingly brief and cryptic queries that users typed into the search field."

The litmus test of the day was searching for the word *university.* In theory, the top search results should have been the home pages for all the major universities. Instead, the search engines retrieved everything that had the word *university* in it—the majority of which were spam pages selling products to students. To help pare down the results, the portals tried to analyze other factors, such as the keyword capitalization, font size, and position. However, it soon became a cat-and-mouse game where websites would put desirable keywords—often in text invisible to the user—throughout their pages to draw in more visitors. Search engines using traditional techniques were now failing.

The Stanford students, though, went about solving the problem in a different way. They made the connection that the links—what users clicked on to navigate through a page—were like the citation pages at the back of their school textbooks. The more a page was referenced, the more credible it likely was. Spam pages, despite having the correct keywords, could be weeded out because no other website would reference them. It was an incredibly simple concept in hindsight, but one that the major portals had missed.

While the idea was simple, in practice, it was far more difficult to manage—although outgoing links were clearly identifiable, what linked *to* a website was not. For the system to work, the students would need to develop a comprehensive map of the internet's link structure. Once complete, it would look like airline routes on a map, whereby the hub cities would instantly stand out.

Mapping the entire internet was a daunting problem. There were already millions of pages on the internet and with only four people on the team, it would take hundreds of years to catalog the backlog of websites by hand, and that wasn't including the hundreds of thousands of pages that were being added daily. The students, though, recognized that clicking on links was a simple task that didn't require much interpretation. This made it a perfect job for an automated application known as a *web crawler*. The crawler would continuously follow and index the links it found, building out the map of the internet. The explosive growth of the internet, instead of a hinderance, would become an asset to the students as the more links the crawler found, the more detail it could add to the map, which in turn would generate better results. Combined with the traditional information retrieval techniques that were already in use, this would allow the BackRub algorithm to outperform the competition in a scalable way.

At the restaurant, the Excite founders began plugging in search queries and were impressed with the results—the students had, in fact, developed a better search tool. It wasn't significantly better, but still, it returned better results. However, after hearing about *how* the algorithm worked, with its back-link structure and web crawlers, the founders knew that this was the future of the internet.

The students were looking to sell the algorithm—the project was becoming a burden to their academic careers, and they wanted to move on from it. They also had no way to monetize it and had already been turned down by several other companies. For $1.6 million, Excite could have it—they would even spend several months at Excite's headquarters integrating it into their existing infrastructure. Their only stipulation was that everything needed to be done before their fall semester so that they could focus on their classes.

It was an incredible deal for Excite. The founders knew that this algorithm would allow Excite to become the only company in the world that could bring order to the internet in a scalable way, allowing them to capture billions of dollars. There was only one problem: the founders didn't have control of their own company.

START-UP

Technology companies compete in one of the most competitive business environments. One of the reasons why is that they heavily leverage computer code, meaning they can scale incredibly fast. The cost to copy additional software once it's been developed is typically far less than a physical product. This means that once an application is developed, everyone can have access to it. This is different from, say, restaurants, where a steak house in New York doesn't see a steak house in Dallas as competition—the cost of time and travel makes one clearly preferable to customers. Both restaurants—even if they're identical—can exist in their own separate ecosystems.

Technology companies, though, must compete in far larger ecosystems. It's a high-risk, high-reward environment whereby the top companies in a field make billions of dollars, the second-tier companies struggle to survive, and the rest go out of business. To compete in this environment, start-ups often go years without generating a profit, sinking tens of millions of dollars into business infrastructure and talent acquisition before hopefully seeing mass adoption and the profits that come with it.

The founders of Excite had a lot in common with the students—in fact, just five years prior, *they* were Stanford students, having developed their skills at the very same computer labs that the students were now using. Back then, they didn't have anywhere near the amount of money required to compete with internet giants such as Yahoo! and America Online. To help solve their cash problem, they turned to a venture capital firm, where they gave up the majority of their company for funding so that they could scale faster.

The venture capital firms were run by highly capable people who had graduated from top schools. However, at the time, they lacked deep expertise of the internet. Their mentality toward leadership was different as well. There wasn't the programmer ethos back then that dominates the leadership of tech companies today. It was believed that, if a company wanted to be taken seriously, a corporate executive, usually Ivy League–trained, should come in and run it—the most famous example being when Apple fired Steve Jobs as the CEO and replaced him with an executive from Pepsi.

As soon as the venture capital firm gained control of Excite, they rebranded it and pushed the founders down the corporate ladder. They then tasked a headhunter agency to find a new CEO—they wanted someone who had an executive presence and who would wear a suit and tie to work instead of the basketball shorts that the founders often wore. They wanted what was known in the industry as "adult supervision" for founders who were in their midtwenties. Their search led them to hiring a man named George Bell.

George was the model CEO of the day. He was Harvard-trained, where he had received an English degree and accolades as a varsity squash player. He had then spent the next decade as a producer for outdoor documentaries, where he traveled the world filming endangered species and vanishing tribes. George had a reputation for being a great pitchman, someone who could get documentaries funded, even while he was out on safari. After traveling as a producer, George had settled down and worked his way up the corporate ladder until he had become the president of a media company.

George believed that partnerships were critical for Excite to maintain relevance. Using the sales skills that he'd developed producing documentaries, he was able to quickly make Excite the exclusive search engine of America Online in exchange for a 20 percent stake of the company. He then struck a seven-year partnership with the financial giant Intuit, maker of Quicken and TurboTax, for another 19 percent stake in Excite. To broaden his user base, he purchased Netbot, a search engine for comparison shopping, and later that year finalized a deal with Ticketmaster to provide direct online ticketing.

George's strategy was a blitzkrieg across the internet, whereby every six to eight weeks, he was acquiring a new company. His view was that the internet was like digital real estate. By controlling valuable areas—such as 10 percent of America Online's home screen—he could then funnel people into Excite's portal, where he could then generate ad revenue. Excite.com would become, as George liked to say, "a one-stop shop for all your needs."

To account for the growing spam problem, George, in the first major consolidation among internet search engines, bought Magellan for $18 million. This gave Excite one of the top website-rating teams, consisting of seventy-five journalists working around the clock to give one-sentence reviews of websites. This helped to bring order to the internet and ensured that Excite.com only had high-quality websites associated with it. So far, they had already amassed over forty thousand reviews.

After the meeting at Fuki Sushi, the founders of Excite had asked George for permission to buy the BackRub algorithm. He denied their request. Excite was already known as one of the best search engines, and in his opinion, after the Magellan acquisition, they had already solved the search problem. The founders disagreed and were able to persuade their venture capital firm to take a second look at the Stanford students. During the meeting, the students, out of options and quickly running out of time, dropped their asking price to $750,000. Excite could have the rights to everything they had developed, so long as they could walk away and go back to their academic careers. The founders were adamant that Excite should take the deal, and although the venture capital firm didn't have a strong preference either way, a meeting was set up between George and the students.

On the day of the meeting, the students arrived at the new Mid-Point Technology Park, home to Excite's headquarters. Entering the eighty-eight-thousand-square-foot glass building, the students made their way to George's office while carrying their computers and presentation materials. After setting up the computers, they started up BackRub in one window and Excite's portal in the other—they would pit the two, head-to-head, to see which one was better.

During the competition, BackRub outpaced Excite's search results, but not by a wide margin. It didn't seem revolutionary. Eventually, George had seen enough; for $750,000, it wasn't worth worrying about—he could acquire the rights, kill a future competitor, and put the technology on a shelf in case they needed it later. However, the students hadn't started the project for the money; they had started it because they saw the potential of the internet and wanted to make it useful. The students had put a clause in the contract that their algorithm needed to be used once it was bought. This proved to be the downfall of the deal. Excite's revenue was generated by people staying within their portal. If they controlled a page, they could market it to advertisers. However, when someone searched for a topic and left their site, they lost that potential user. The website's *stickiness*, as it's called, was one of the most important metrics of the day, and George believed that if a search engine was "too good," it could be counterproductive. This, combined with his belief that the search problem had been tamed, led him to reject the deal.

ANTI-PORTAL

For the next year and a half, every company the students approached also turned them down. "We couldn't get anyone interested," said one of the students. "We did get offers, but they weren't for much money, so we said, 'Whatever,' and went back to Stanford to work on it some more." The students eventually developed BackRub into the anti-portal—instead of hundreds of links and advertisements across their home screen, they pared everything down until there was only a small search box and two buttons on the screen. In part, it was because they didn't have the resources to add anything else, but more so, it was because it allowed the website to load faster—which, early on, had become one of their core principles.

Since that meeting in the winter of 1997, the internet landscape has changed dramatically. Excite soon merged with @Home Network in a $6.7 billion blockbuster deal, becoming the largest merger of two internet companies at the time. Within two years, though, the conglomerate imploded under massive losses, causing a 90 percent drop in stock value and forcing them to file for bankruptcy. The company was then broken up and sold at discount prices to its former competitors.

The students continued to invest in search—everything they did was about making it more efficient for users, regardless of how sticky their website was. Eventually, they cracked the revenue problem by developing a system whereby advertisers auctioned to be associated with keywords that users search for. As one of the few companies in the world that could tame the internet, they grew with it. Hoping to turn their project into a business, they decided to rename their algorithm. While serious consideration was given to the name "the Whatbox," they eventually changed their name from BackRub to a play on the mathematical term for one followed by one hundred zeros and called themselves Google. Today, Google—founded by the former Stanford students Larry Page and Sergey Brin—is worth over $1.5 trillion.

There's no way to tell whether Excite would have gone on to be as successful as Google if George had bought the students' algorithm that day. However, passing on it is now considered one of the worst business decisions in history, one that eventually contributed to the company's collapse. The root cause is that George didn't understand power laws on a deep enough level and how they related to the problems he was facing. He didn't see how the exponential growth of the internet would radically alter the system within which he was working. Hiring teams of journalists to review websites was a linear solution. This can work for books, movies, and products where there are very few compared to the overall user base. However, the internet gave anyone with a computer the ability to make a website within a few hours. This created a staggering growth in the number of websites. It's understandable why he missed it—in 1997, the internet hadn't hit the knee in the curve yet. It's like the penny example on day ten—if you zoom in closely enough, the graph looks linear. However, within a few years, it grew dramatically. Today, if a company like Excite were to manually review websites, they would need well over one hundred thousand journalists.

There was, however, an even more fundamental power law that web portals of the late 1990s failed to account for. Pioneered by Robert Metcalfe, one of the early inventors of the Ethernet, the power law, known as Metcalfe's Law, states that the value of a network grows exponentially with the total number of users. Think of a telephone—if you were the only one in the world who had one, it would be worthless. Even if a few people had one, it still wouldn't provide much value. However, because the majority of people own phones, they're incredibly valuable. The same is true of social media, dating apps, and even the internet itself. Web portals were a bottleneck that limited the number of connections that users could make. It was a linear solution that turned the internet into just a digital newspaper. Because the internet was so new, most users were happy with the status quo. Google's search engine, however, removed the bottleneck and gave users access to the full power of the internet while still being controllable. This caused users to rapidly adopt Google's search engine and resulted in the collapse of the web portals. The network effect is so powerful that today it can often account for 70 percent or more of the value of a digital company.

POWER LAWS

Power laws govern the world around us. They're extensively used in physics, engineering, biology, psychology, economics, meteorology, criminology, and many other fields. In biology, for instance, Kleiber's law demonstrates that an animal's metabolism doesn't scale linearly with its size but rather adheres to a power law. For example, a cat, despite weighing over one hundred times more than a mouse, only requires thirty-two times the energy to sustain itself. It's a form of economies of scale whereby a doubling of the size doesn't require a doubling of the energy consumption. This law surprisingly holds true throughout much of the animal kingdom—the same is true for a cow, which is one hundred times heavier than a cat, and a whale, which is one hundred times heavier than a cow. And because life span is closely related to metabolism, this power law is why a mouse only lives a few years while a whale can live more than eighty years (humans, through health care and technology, now live significantly longer than our size would predict).

Being able to quickly identify a variable as adhering to a power law is critical during the assessment phase of the ACE Helix. It allows us to prioritize the key points that will most affect our decision. While there are hundreds of specific power laws throughout nearly every known field, we can simplify all of them down to just three generic types, allowing us to quickly prioritize our cross-check.

1. Exponential Growth

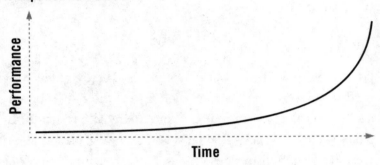

Exponential growth describes how populations increase, how viruses spread, how compound interest grows, how computer processing power is increasing, and much more. Exponential growth means that as a quantity increases, the rate at which it grows also increases. The growth is accelerating over time. In graph form, exponential growth looks like a *J*—the quantity starts off by increasing slowly and then rapidly takes off. An easy way to identify exponential growth is seeing if there's a consistent doubling time. If it takes a city ten years to grow from ten thousand to twenty thousand residents and then another ten years to grow from twenty thousand to forty thousand and so on, it's growing exponentially.

A technique to quickly calculate exponential growth is called the *rule of seventy.* By dividing seventy by the growth rate, you can find the doubling time. For instance, say your investments are growing by 7 percent each year. By dividing seventy by seven, you can quickly see that your money will double every ten years.

2. Diminishing Returns

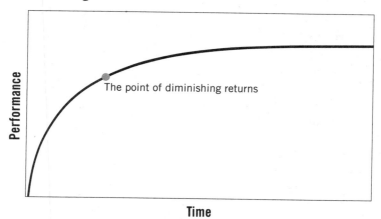

The point of diminishing returns

The law of diminishing returns can be used to describe many relationships, from why supercars are incredibly expensive to why only a small amount of detergent is needed when washing your clothes. *Diminishing returns* refers to a situation in which a smaller result is achieved for an increasing amount of resources and effort. A graph of diminishing returns quickly climbs but then tapers off. In some cases, it can eventually decrease and turn into negative returns.

Take a restaurant with only one cook. If the restaurant's busy, then having only one cook is likely a bottleneck for the operation. Hiring more cooks will unlock additional capacity for the restaurant. Each new cook hired increases the amount of food the restaurant can serve, but, at some point, at a smaller and smaller rate. Based on the cost of each cook, there comes a point where it's not economically viable to hire additional cooks. Even without factoring in cost, eventually the kitchen is so full of people that, even if the labor is free, hiring new cooks will impede progress and result in a negative return.

3. Long Tail

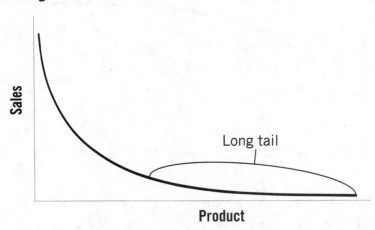

The long-tail power law forms the basis for the economist Vilfredo Pareto's famous 80–20 rule, where he noticed that 20 percent of the people in Italy owned 80 percent of the land. This idea, that a large percentage of the impact and results are generated by a small percentage of the work, has since been found in corporation sizes, income rankings, TV show viewers, city populations, and even the RNA coding in our cells. A graph of a long-tail power law starts high and then rapidly decreases but at a smaller and smaller amount, eventually creating what looks like a long tail as it approaches zero.

For example, named after George Zipf, Zipf's law shows that the most frequent word used in a language will occur twice as often as the second-most-frequent word, three times as often as the third-most-frequent word, and so on. In the English language, *the* is the most frequent word used and accounts for nearly 5 percent of all words, followed by *of,* which accounts for just over 3.5 percent, and then *and,* which accounts for 2.4 percent. It's a surprisingly consistent law that holds true throughout nearly all languages. The takeaway for a new speaker is that by just learning the top 135 words of a language, they can speak half of all the words used by a native speaker.

TIPPING POINTS

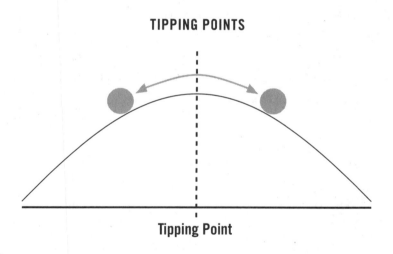

Tipping Point

In addition to power laws, there are often areas in a system where a small change in the input can disproportionately affect the output. These tipping points are critical moments when a minor change can make a major difference. Think of water, for instance: the difference between 33 degrees Fahrenheit and 31 degrees Fahrenheit doesn't feel that different, but it can turn water into ice. The old proverb of the straw that broke the camel's back is an example of this. As weight is loaded onto the camel, eventually a tiny amount of weight causes a massive change to the camel's health.

Tipping points can be found in every field and are often difficult for us to conceptualize because they represent extreme forms of nonlinear behavior. Even if we know there's a tipping point, if we haven't experienced it firsthand, then it can often be difficult to reconcile our past experiences with what we've been taught. We become accustomed to how our actions are affecting a system, and then suddenly, the outcome is much different from what we were expecting. This is what ultimately led to me putting the F-16 out of control. At the time, I didn't realize how important it was to cross-check my airspeed before matching the adversary in the vertical. I—incorrectly—assumed that being slightly slow would have a small impact on the outcome.

OUT OF CONTROL

The nose of my F-16 continued slicing through the air, violently throwing me and everything not strapped down around the cockpit. It felt like I was in the jaws of a giant animal trying to rip me apart. I looked up from the ejection handle—I had wanted to make sure I knew exactly where it was so that I could spend the rest of the time gaining control of the aircraft. I then focused my eyes on my altitude while beginning the out of control recovery checklist that I had memorized during my training: I released pressure on the stick, pulled the throttle to idle, and reset the flight control computers.

The nose of the F-16, however, continued to slice through

the air like a leaf falling from a tree. I moved on to the next steps. With my left hand, I found the manual-pitch-override switch, which would allow me to override the flight controls and control them manually. While holding the switch, I began pushing the stick down every time the nose fell and pulling back every time it rose—like rocking a car out of a snowbank.

Eventually, the nose of the jet fell through. I was now pointed straight down, but still well below flying speed. Hanging from my shoulder straps, I could see the mountains and trees rapidly growing closer. I slammed the throttle forward, activating max afterburner, and quickly accelerated until I was fast enough to pull back on the stick. I felt the g-forces increase, causing me to sink into the seat while the nose of the jet carved upward. Eventually, my flight path leveled out. I recovered the jet, though only several thousand feet above the mountains. Not understanding power laws and tipping points had almost cost me my life.

FINDING THEM

Now that we have a better understanding of nonlinear behavior and power laws, the next question is: How can we better identify them when assessing a problem? The first step is to increase our awareness of our linear bias. We are naturally programmed to view the world in a linear way. For much of history, mistakenly identifying a power law as a linear relationship wasn't a big deal because the world wasn't nearly as leveraged. Today, though, our decisions are greatly leveraged by technology. Each decision we make is amplified to produce a far greater outcome than we could produce on our own. For example, in the past, a village of fishermen didn't have to worry nearly as much about overfishing a body of water. Their tools limited the impact they could make. However, today, a small fleet of modern mega-trawlers can quickly collapse an entire ecosystem within a few years if left unchecked.

The next step to fighting linear bias is to graph the data. Raw numbers are abstract and difficult for humans to process. However, by graphing them, patterns often emerge. We can quickly turn discrete points of data into an understanding of the system. This can often help people to arrive at the correct solution on their own. For instance, researchers found that people tend to incorrectly estimate the time saved when increasing their driving speed. That's because the most prominent information shown to them is their speed, which, because of linear bias, leads them to believe that it's linearly correlated. However, it actually adheres to a long-tail power law. Increasing your speed from forty to sixty-five will save you about six minutes every ten miles but going from sixty-five to ninety will only save about half the time despite the same speed increase. This misconception often leads people to unnecessarily speed, causing poor fuel consumption and more accidents. The researchers, however, found that they could remove this bias by adding an extra dial they called a "paceometer," which showed how long it would take drivers to travel ten miles. This allowed people to far more accurately estimate their time saved and better prioritize speed versus safety and fuel consumption.

Another way to see if there's a power law within a system

is to use extreme data points. Any graph can look linear if zoomed in enough. However, by zooming out, it can quickly become evident that a relationship isn't linear. Take someone trying to demonstrate the power of compound interest. Instead of a 5–10 percent rate of return, make it 100 percent, and instead of yearly, make it daily. This is the penny example from earlier, which dramatically shows the impact of exponential growth. Once you understand there's a power law at play, you can refine the solution by using more realistic numbers.

Each step of the ACE Helix builds on top of the last. A proper assessment of the problem is the foundation of good decision-making. It's impossible to consistently make good decisions without it. A proper assessment doesn't necessarily need to take a lot of time; often, it can be made in just seconds. However, it needs to be practiced to the point where it becomes second nature.

LEARNED LESSONS

Nangarhar Province, Afghanistan: 1730 Local Time

After several hours of armed overwatch in southern Afghanistan, my wingman and I now found ourselves racing across the country in our F-16s to support a convoy of U.S. Army Rangers who had just come under attack and were now pinned down. The convoy had been returning from a clearing mission when ISIS fighters began engaging them with automatic fire. After their prolonged mission, the Rangers were now low on resources and without air cover. With nightfall quickly approaching, we needed to destroy the ISIS fighters immediately or word would soon get out that U.S. forces were in trouble, allowing ISIS to mobilize reinforcements throughout the region.

Flying at maximum speed, we were overhead within minutes and began coordinating with the Rangers. Over the radio, they requested immediate attacks on several of the ISIS machine-gun emplacements. Once we found the targets, my wingman and I began dropping five-hundred-pound GPS-guided bombs—each one taking out individual machine-gun nests. This enabled the troops to slowly start maneuvering around the enemy. Soon, we were out of bombs, and with enemy snipers still engaging the Rangers, we turned to our laser rockets—one of the newest weapons in our inventory.

The laser rockets, originally designed for helicopters, had just been approved for fighters, and we were one of the first squadrons to ever use them. In fact, most of us hadn't even heard of them until midway through our combat spin-up, when it was announced that there would be hundreds waiting for us once we deployed. That set off a scramble for us to figure out how to employ them. Our avionics didn't even have an ability to load them into the aircraft—we had to trick the jet's computer by loading them into the avionics as old, unguided bombs. The rockets, though, were unique in that, once fired, they could be continuously guided by a laser on board our aircraft. Combined with our targeting pods, which allowed us to zoom in to targets from miles away, this produced a lethal combination that was perfect for engaging the enemy in Afghanistan.

I began to employ the laser rockets—for each shot, I dived toward the target, hit the red weapon release button—known as the *pickle button*—and watched the rocket streak off from my wing. I then pulled up from the dive and guided the rocket into the target using a cursor on the throttle. The rockets were "nail drivers," as we called them; they almost always hit the target, which we referred to as a *shack*.

By now, the sun was setting, turning the dusty atmosphere

into a deep, hazy red. A storm was beginning to form with pockets of dense, low-level clouds that were merging inside the valley we were operating in. Combined with the ten-thousand-foot mountains surrounding us, this created a strange other-worldly landscape. After several rocket passes, my aircraft was Remington, meaning the only weapon I had left was the gun—a relic from a previous era that we only used as a last resort.

Employing smart weapons is highly procedural, and as a pilot, you're primarily concerned with managing the systems to make sure that you satisfy all the numerous checks to employ the weapons. Though it takes a lot of focus and skill, the flying portion is not especially demanding. The gun, however, requires stick-and-rudder skills—more so than perhaps any other maneuver. It requires getting close to the enemy near the unforgiving ground and then having a certain feel of the jet so that you can roll in and shoot an accurate burst. There's also a surprising amount of academic theory and math behind the tactic, making it one of the most difficult skills to master. To become good at strafing, a pilot needs to develop a strong academic understanding of the tactic so that they can quickly account for changing conditions in the air. They then need to turn this understanding into flying intuition so that it becomes second nature when called on.

I remember being lost in my first academic class on strafing and unguided bomb deliveries. I had expected it to be like shooting a handgun: You point at the target and pull the trigger. However, because of the speeds we fly, the geometry turned out to be complex. Not only did we have to account for the trajectory of the bullets we were shooting, but we also had to account for our own dive angle and speed, which often approached six hundred miles per hour. And getting the bullets onto the target was only half of the maneuver; the second half was safely pulling out of the dive, which often brought us to just one hundred feet above the ground. Each weapon that we carried had a different funnel that we had to precisely fly through to employ it. If our dive angle was too steep, we would end up being too high to be effective and would also have trouble pulling up from the dive. If we were too shallow, we would be too low and could crash into the terrain. Even if we set the angle perfectly, we could either be on what's known as a *high wire* or *low wire*, which would both negatively affect the pass—meaning we would need to offset our original dive angle. And because a bullet or bomb was leaving the aircraft and falling to the ground, we also had to account for the changing relationship between our aircraft, which was flying straight, and the weapon, which would immediately begin arcing.

Once my class had a thorough understanding of the concepts, we began learning mental shortcuts, known as *heuristics,* that allowed us to quickly set up the correct parameters. One of the most useful was a concept known as *canopy codes.* By flying perpendicularly to a target, we could wait until the target lined up on a specific point on our canopy before rolling in. This allowed us to set the angle perfectly regardless of our altitude or distance. It was a great technique; however, the canopy of the F-16 made it more difficult to learn than in other aircraft.

One of the best features of the F-16 is its bubble canopy—it provides a near 360-degree view around the pilot. It's such a good view that when we fly, we don't say we're strapping into the aircraft but rather that we're strapping the jet on our backs because the canopy gives the illusion that you're floating in air. The downside is that there are no physical marks on it to reference—you have to imagine where they would be. As students, we sometimes drew marks on the canopy with a grease pencil. We then progressed to using our outstretched hands to measure the distance from the target to the bottom of the canopy—for my sitting height, it was a little more than a fist and a thumb above the canopy rail. But eventually, after hundreds of times strafing, it became automatic. Between the academics, the heuristics, and the practice, we had built an interlocked understanding that became an extension of our instincts to the point where we didn't have to think about it.

AFGHANISTAN

Now that it was getting darker, I began to see muzzle flashes from the guns of the ISIS fighters as they continued shooting at the Rangers. I dove to a lower altitude and tightened my orbit around the target. The clouds were now becoming a factor. I was in the middle of a valley with mountains rising far above me on two sides—if I went into a cloud, I could easily wind up slamming into the side of a mountain. That meant instead of a stable orbit, I had to maneuver around the dense clouds—climbing and descending while continually changing my distance from the target. Since seeing the first muzzle flash, I hadn't taken my eyes off the enemy—I didn't want to lose sight of them in the tree line they were concealed behind. That meant that I couldn't align the F-16's sensors to the target—this would be a fully manual pass relying on the flying instincts I had built up over the years.

Now that I was lower, I could see that in addition to mountains on both sides, just past the target, there was rising terrain. After my strafing run, I would be pointed toward one of the mountains and would need to thread the needle through a gap in the ridgeline. Even though the F-16 is one of the best-turning fighters in the world, because of its high speed, its flight path arcs through the sky, as opposed to tightly turning like in a car. This means that when flying the Viper, you have to anticipate far in advance where the aircraft will be; otherwise, you can easily crash into the ground.

I didn't have time to calculate the geometry, and even if I did, it wouldn't have been accurate enough because of how complex and dynamic the situation was. For instance, I would have had to calculate my turn radius to ensure I could clear the mountains, but that wouldn't have been available without a detailed sight survey. Heuristics alone wouldn't have worked either—the target was at a high elevation, meaning the jet's engine and turn performance would be decreased. My fuel was low, decreasing my weight and increasing my maneuverability. There were also strong headwinds, which I would have to compensate for with my dive angle. Only by merging an academic understanding along with the heuristics and then practicing the maneuver over and over did I have the necessary tools to solve the tactical problem. The training that the Air Force had put me through had created the necessary mental framework where all of that became intuitive—I could see in my mind the exact path I needed to take to avoid the mountains and how close I would get to the terrain as I climbed back into my orbit.

Once I was lined up between the mountains, I pushed the throttle into military power, rolling the jet inverted while pulling the nose of the aircraft toward the target until it was in the middle of my heads-up display. Simultaneously, I pushed a button on the throttle, activating the strafe mode of the jet, which called up the aiming reticle. I was now diving toward the target, accelerating past five hundred miles per hour. As the range rapidly counted down, I lined up the center dot of the reticle over the target. Once I was in firing range, I squeezed the trigger. Almost instantaneously, the six-barrel Gatling gun began violently shaking the plane, blurring everything I was looking at from the force on my eyes. I was now unleashing six thousand rounds per minute toward the target—each round a 20 mm high-explosive incendiary shell that would have the effect of a small grenade. After a several-second burst, I released the trigger and pulled back on the stick. I could feel the g-force pushing me into the seat as I watched the rounds impact along the tree line. Flying directly above the enemy, I could see that in addition to the ISIS fighters in the tree line, there were also two fortified machine-gun emplacements.

The rising terrain made the recovery challenging—it was almost the same gradient as my recovery, which meant as I climbed, I continued to stay the same distance above the ground. I turned toward the gap in the ridgeline and increased my pull, feeling my mask press down on my face. Finally, I passed through it, the rock walls quickly falling below my aircraft as I climbed back to my orbit.

Over the radio, the troops confirmed that the strafing pass was successful; I had taken out the fighters in the middle, leaving only the machine-gun emplacements. The Rangers, however, were still taking fire and requested another immediate pass. A minute later, I rolled back in. I could see the intricate tree line with built-in trenches protecting the ISIS fighters. Once I was within range, I squeezed the trigger, activating the gun and shaking the plane so violently that yellow insulation dust from inside the aircraft covered my left shoulder. I released the trigger, and a moment later, I could see the rounds impacting the western machine-gun nest as I climbed through the gap in the ridgeline again. Simultaneously, my jet's fuel alarm went off as the word *BINGO* flashed in my HUD—I was now at my minimum fuel for getting back to the tanker.

Our sprint across Afghanistan had burned a significant amount of our fuel. Our tanker—a specially designed plane that allows us to refuel in the air—had finally caught back up to us and had set up an orbit fifty miles to the north. Typically, as fighter aircraft, we always travel as a team for mutual support. That way, if anything happens, there's another pilot to back you up. However, in this case, due to the troops under fire, I had already sent my wingman off to the tanker on his own—a tactic called *yo-yo ops,* which allowed us to maintain continuous coverage over the Rangers.

By now, my wingman had just finished refueling and was still ten minutes away from rejoining the fight. With the sun already below the horizon, it was quickly getting dark outside. Normally, strafing at night is possible—although significantly more difficult with the added complexity of seeing the world through night vision goggles—however, due to the extreme terrain and poor weather, it would be impossible tonight. Out of bombs and rockets, there was only time for one final strafing pass.

BINGO

In pilot training, you're taught to never change your minimum fuel, known as *bingo fuel*. Once you hit it, you immediately start flying back to base. Over the years, many pilots have reset it only to have forgotten about it or miscalculated it and run out of fuel. This, however, was a more complex situation than pilot training. We were the only aircraft on station, we were out of bombs and rockets, and with night setting in, we would soon lose the ability to help the troops under fire.

I had been on the advance team for the deployment and had flown out a week ahead of the rest of the squadron. Our job was to set up everything so that as soon as the squadron arrived, we were ready to start flying missions. One of the documents that my team had created was a "bingo map" so that no matter where a pilot was in the country, they could easily see how much fuel they needed to get home. In calculating the map, we had to make assumptions such as the weapons the aircraft was carrying, how fast it was flying, the altitude of flight, windspeed, and other factors. Because I had helped make the map, I knew that it was slightly conservative and that as long as I flew an aggressive maximum-range profile to the tanker, I would have enough fuel for one last strafing pass.

With that, I turned off my bingo alarm and told the troops I would be in for one final strafing pass. As I made my way around the orbit, the darkness was starting to make it difficult to see. It would have been too dangerous to strafe if this had been my first attempt, but having done it twice before, I knew what to expect. Now, as I rolled in, I began to see muzzle fire from the remaining machine-gun nest—they were shooting at my aircraft. Although the ISIS fighters were most likely only equipped with small arms and rocket-propelled grenades—what we classified as a low threat—there's always a chance of a round hitting a critical part of the aircraft and bringing it down. This was particularly true now that my aircraft was pointed straight at them and rapidly closing the range between us.

Unlike aircraft such as the A-10 with armor to protect the pilot as well as other critical parts of the aircraft, the F-16's survival is entirely dependent on its speed and maneuverability. The jet was built to be as light as possible, which means it had to sacrifice any excess weight, including armor. It's an effective trade-off for dogfights and missiles at altitude; however, the aircraft's protection is not well suited for flying close to the ground, where anyone with a rifle can get a lucky shot off. In fact, just the year before my squadron's arrival, a lucky shot from a Taliban fighter had hit a missile on an F-16's wing, causing it to ignite and putting the aircraft in an extreme yaw. Fortunately, the missile's safety system prevented it from detonating; however, it was a clear reminder that even a small bullet—known to fighter pilots as *the golden bb*—can bring down an entire aircraft.

As the gray tree line rapidly grew in my canopy, I began to make out the machine-gun nest where the fire was coming from. I lined up my aiming reticle on the source of the gunfire and pulled back on the trigger. The gun once again spun to life as it discharged the rounds downrange. Soon thereafter, I could see the explosions impacting the enemy position as each round detonated, creating a field of fire. I held the trigger down until the shaking inside the jet stopped, signaling I was out of bullets—I was now out of every weapon onboard my aircraft. I pulled back hard on the stick, carving through the gap in the mountain. This time, I stayed low, below one thousand feet as I accelerated on a fuel-conservation flight profile. Once I hit 500 knots, or 575 miles per hour, I then rapidly climbed into the air on what's called a *sky hook* toward the tanker. Over the radio, I could hear the controller saying, "Good hits, good hits! We've stopped taking fire."

RED FLAG

When flying a fighter, there isn't time to think through all the decisions that need to be made. The flying is so complex and the speeds so fast that most of the decision-making process needs to become instinctual. The challenge is that flying a jet is a vastly different experience from everyday life. No one is born a good pilot. In fact, most fighter pilots show up to pilot training with zero flight experience. That means their instincts must quickly be built from the ground up before they're called on to use them during an actual mission. It's a delicate balance of resources and risk to ensure we have the most capable fighter pilots in the world.

One of the defining moments for U.S. fighter pilots was the establishment of a training exercise called Red Flag. Red Flag was born out of the Vietnam War, where fighter pilots were being shot down at an unacceptably high rate. This led to a series of secret studies conducted by the U.S. Air Force called Project Red Baron, named after the famed World War I ace. Declassified only in 2001, the Project Red Baron studies demonstrated that U.S. pilots were inadequately trained for combat. They identified that senior leaders, out of a fear of causing accidents, had severely restricted the types of training missions the pilots could fly. This led to pilots being required to fly the same scripted flights over and over again, atrophying their decision-making ability. When they deployed to Vietnam, they had difficulty adapting to the dynamic nature of aerial combat. The problems were especially acute for pilots before they had a chance to fly their first ten combat missions, after which the survival rate dramatically climbed. Red Flag, therefore, was started to give pilots realistic training so that they could regain their ability to make decisive decisions during the fog and friction of war.

Pilots from around the country would meet at Nellis Air Force Base in Las Vegas to train over the remote Nevada desert. There they had a chance to fly realistic missions, bridging the gap between their everyday training and the complexities of actually going to war. Over the years, Red Flag eventually grew into the Air Force's premier combat exercise. Dedicated aggressor squadrons were established to replicate enemy tactics,

while captured enemy equipment was used to further enhance the realism. Once the missions ended, they would be
digitally rendered so that the pilots could develop lessons on
how they could perform better. It became such a success that
it's now permanently held several times a year and expanded
from just an Air Force exercise to all military branches, as
well as to many other countries, and is now regarded as the
most comprehensive training exercise in the world.

My first time attending a Red Flag was several years into
flying the F-16. My squadron took off from the East Coast
and flew across the country, refueling several times from an
airborne tanker along the way. As we flew over Nellis Air
Force Base, I looked down and could see hundreds of other
aircraft of all shapes and sizes parked wing to wing, covering
the entire base. It was a chaotic scene that looked like a mall
parking lot on Christmas Eve, only with some of the most
advanced aircraft in the world. After landing, we received our
parking spots over the radio and navigated through the con-
gestion of other aircraft and maintainers who were preparing
for the upcoming exercise.

Over the next few weeks, we flew dozens of simulated combat missions. It was an incredible experience to be a part of
training at the highest level. It was a learning laboratory where
no expense was spared at turning us into the best fighter pilots.
Intermixed with some of the younger pilots such as myself
were seasoned pilots who had decades of experience flying
fighters. The flights themselves were overwhelming—despite
having flown the F-16 for several years, the complexity of
executing as such a large force against teams of adversaries
that were well prepared and at their home base was challeng-

ing. The debriefs after the missions were equally demanding. Though we would only fly for about an hour and a half, we would then spend the next eight hours breaking down and analyzing the missions, looking at everything we could improve upon. For night missions, that often meant walking out of the windowless, secure debriefing facilities with the sun well above the horizon. Overall, it was a humbling experience—if it had been a real combat scenario, I would have died several times over.

Over the years, I've had a chance to attend nearly a dozen similar exercises. Each exercise was challenging, and as my skills grew, my responsibilities grew as well. After learning how to fly as a wingman, I was promoted to a flight lead, where I was in charge of four F-16s. I then became a team lead, where I was responsible for planning a portion of the mission while leading a few dozen aircraft. Eventually, I became the mission commander, tasked with planning and leading the entire mission, consisting of nearly one hundred other aircraft.

One mission that stands out was the rescue of a pilot who had been shot down the day before. As the overall commander, it was my job to lead a hundred other pilots, along with several hundred support personnel, to develop a plan to recover the downed pilot. Everything from the taxi sequence and airborne refueling to the tactics and egress had to be planned down to the smallest detail, along with contingency plans for when things went wrong.

On the day of the mission, I was the first fighter airborne, and for the next thirty minutes, aircraft continuously took off from the base so we could amass the necessary firepower to go deep into enemy territory and protect the helicopters as they made their way in to rescue the downed pilot.

No plan survives first contact with the enemy—the enemy was jamming the radio frequencies, making it difficult to communicate with the downed pilot. This delayed our ability to accurately locate him—all the while we continued to wait, quickly burning our fuel.

Eventually, we got to the point where we had to execute; otherwise, the F-22s—my most capable air-to-air fighters—wouldn't be able to stay on station for the full duration of the mission. However, we still hadn't located the downed pilot, meaning there would be a large amount of uncertainty and risk if we chose to proceed with the mission. This gave me three options: execute and hope we could find the downed pilot on the way in, continue waiting and lose F-22 coverage at the end of the mission, or fully abort the mission.

As the commander, I was responsible for the decision. There were really only two feasible options—either go or abort. Having only partial air coverage would guarantee mission failure if the enemy sent up a sizable force like our intelligence expected. I chose to be aggressive and execute the mission. With that, we pushed into enemy territory. The F-22s immediately began engaging and shooting down the enemy fighters while the F-16s I was leading destroyed the surface-to-air missile sites. The rest of the fighters, along with several B-2 stealth bombers, who had been airborne for over five hours crossing the country to participate in the mission, hit key targets, disabling the enemy's ability to communicate and control their forces.

Meanwhile, the helicopters slowly made their way into

enemy territory, attempting to contact the downed pilot. However, in addition to the radios being jammed, their low altitude made it difficult for them to pick up the beacon that the pilot was carrying. This caused the helicopters to fly slightly off course on their way to rescue the pilot. By the time they located him, they were ten minutes behind the timeline.

Eventually, the helicopters picked up the pilot and began slowly making their way back. However, the F-22s soon hit their bingo fuel and were forced to return to their base. Despite a valiant effort by my remaining fighters, an enemy aircraft was able to make it through our defenses and shoot down one of the helicopters.

As the mission commander, I had failed to rescue the downed pilot. Not only that, there were now additional airmen in enemy territory, creating an even bigger problem for follow-on missions. Once the flight was over, it was my job to lead the hundreds of people who had participated in the exercise through all the decisions I had made and what I could improve upon. In this case, there were several poor decisions that had compounded on top of each other to cause the mission to fail. First, I should have allocated a formation of aircraft flying at a higher altitude to attempt to contact the downed pilot. This would have prevented many of the communication problems the helicopters had at low altitude. Second, I should have built in a longer buffer for the time it would take the helicopters to pick up the downed pilot. I had built the timing based on everything going right. However, if I had studied similar missions in the past, I would have seen that there was often a 10–15 percent delay. Lastly, I chose to execute the mission even though I didn't have contact with the downed pilot. This exceeded the acceptable level of risk for the mission—our goal was to rescue an airman, not to leave more out on the battlefield. As soon as the F-22s hit their bingo fuel, I should have aborted the mission.

These experiences at Red Flag as well as other large exercises helped hone my decision-making under uncertainty and pressure. For each mission, I would write down the top lessons I had learned in a small notebook that I always kept in my flight suit pocket. Before each flight, I would review similar missions and strive to repeat what I had done well and not make mistakes that I had made in the past. This continual iteration helped to develop my decision-making to the point where much of it became second nature, allowing me to focus on higher-level decisions that I hadn't been able to think about before. Like the founders of Red Flag intended, the missions had given me the opportunity to learn the lessons in a training environment so that by the time I deployed to combat, many of them were automatic.

APPLICATION

The **Choose** phase of the ACE Helix comes down to learning how the problems we're facing connect to our end objectives. Humans are naturally good at learning; our superpower isn't strength or speed or size. The history of our evolution is notable for two things: The first is the decline in our strength over the years, and the second is the growth in both the size and complexity of our brains. Today, our brains are nearly seven times larger than a similarly sized mammal's. Even for primates, who have the most efficiently packaged brains, our brains are still three times larger than expected. In a sense, nature went all in on optimizing for our brains at the expense of everything else.

Our brains are undeniably powerful compared to those of other animals; however, our raw intelligence only tells part of the story. It's our ability to systemize lessons and then share that information throughout our network that has allowed us to far outstrip our biology. This has allowed us to specialize and become experts. Initially, it was specialization among tribes. By not having to do everything needed for survival, we could spend time innovating. These early seeds of innovation caused a growth in human knowledge that has compounded over the years. Today, we're not making tools that are ten times better than those made by other animals; we're making ones that are millions of times better—satellites, stealth aircraft, and augmented reality devices are incomprehensibly advanced compared to the tools and technology used by the rest of the animal kingdom.

As fighter pilots, our focus for the last fifty years has been on understanding how to harness this superpower to outlearn our adversaries. Although our brains are fantastic learning machines, the way we process experiences into lessons can still be greatly improved. Through combat as well as exercises such as Red Flag, we've had a chance to develop several principles for teaching information so that it's actionable and can be quickly recalled in a dynamic environment.

To help illustrate the steps of the process, I'll share a story from an important transition that occurred within the U.S. Air Force. In 2017, the F-35 was finally ready to scale from a preproduction test aircraft to a full combat-ready platform. Up to that point, only highly experienced pilots who had flown another fighter—such as the F-16, F-15, A-10, and F-22—were eligible to fly the aircraft. However, with production ramping up, it was important to bring in new pilots who could provide continuity to the program once the more experienced pilots retired.

Because the F-35 was such a radical departure from previous fighter designs, the training for new pilots needed to be developed from scratch. At the same time, the experienced instructor pilots developing the training all came from different fighter aircraft, each with their own cultures that prioritized different aspects of what makes a great fighter pilot. The stakes were high—the F-35 program was expected to be the most expensive weapons program in history, at a cost of over $1.5 trillion, and was to become the backbone of U.S. airpower for the next several decades. It was a tremendous opportunity— one that had never occurred at this scale in the history of air combat. The central question was: How do we teach pilots to be as capable as possible in the shortest amount of time given our resource constraints?

Like the way we plan missions, we started with the end objective and worked backward. For new students out of pilot training, we wanted an F-35 wingman who could survive and thrive against advanced adversaries well into the 2030s. For seasoned pilots coming from previous fighters, we wanted to keep their valuable experience while updating their understanding of air combat to account for the revolutionary changes that came with the F-35. To do that, we utilized several principles for teaching and learning. Although these principles were developed for training fighter pilots, their reach goes beyond aviation and can be adapted for many other areas.

1. Concepts over facts

Learning is about being able to forecast the future. By understanding the cause-and-effect relationship of the world around us, we can make decisions that will have the highest probability of accomplishing our objectives. This allows us to rapidly assess the world around us, choose the correct solution, and then execute.

A robust mental framework that can accommodate many different scenarios is challenging and goes beyond just memorizing facts. There are many people who are smart, are well educated, and have memorized large amounts of information and numerous facts but who lack a broad understanding of the consequences of their decisions. Many of them are quite capable, but only for a narrow set of conditions. They lack the ability to think clearly, which is far more valuable in the real world than raw intelligence. Once the conditions they're used to seeing change, sometimes even by a minute amount, they often make spectacularly wrong decisions.

Combat, however, is one of the most dynamic and demanding environments in the world. Countries dedicate tremendous resources and talent toward countering adversaries. Any perceived weakness is targeted, often from an asymmetric axis. As fighter pilots, we might be attacked from the air, but we also might be attacked from ground-based missiles, electronic jamming, cyberattacks, or even enemy snipers or improvised explosive devices before we even get to the cockpit. During one of my assignments, we were briefed that a threat country had dossiers for each fighter pilot stationed in the area, and should a war start, we would likely be targeted by assassins.

To produce dynamic and flexible thinkers, we needed to start by building a robust mental framework that would be comprised of general concepts and reinforced with lessons learned through experience. We then gradually added more detailed information, but only as it supported the overall framework.

One of the problems we had was that modern fighter aircraft are incredibly complex—the F-35 has over eight million lines of code and thousands of different submenus and avionics settings, meaning pilots had far more to learn than ever before. The natural inclination was to teach students through traditional methods—lectures, readings, and tests—which, while it would have been the fastest way to impart the knowledge to them, wouldn't have enabled them to rapidly recall relevant information to solve complex problems. We needed the information to become an intuitive part of their thought process.

To do that, we prioritized concepts over facts—at every opportunity, we emphasized a deep understanding of how different systems interacted and how it pertained to the decisions they needed to make. For example, students didn't need to know the specific terminology or the precise numbers associated with an enemy's missile system, but they needed to understand how their aircraft would be targeted and the steps they needed to take to defend themselves. Information was only useful if it could be used to make better and quicker decisions. While numbers and terminology are quick to change, concepts typically evolve much more slowly.

One way of visualizing this method of learning is by picturing a tree. Trees begin with a trunk that gradually splits off into thinner and thinner branches. Eventually, at the end of the smallest branches are leaves. Any leaves that aren't attached fall to the ground and are useless to the tree. In our learning model, the leaves were the facts, or bits of information, while the trunk and the branches represented the concepts. Every fact needed to be tied to a concept. We didn't want students who were simply good at multiple choice tests; we wanted them to use the information to be the best pilots possible.

By pooling the top training techniques from each fighter community, we were able to implement underlying principles for how people learn best. The first was establishing the *why* of the information being taught. This served to weave the information into a singular and overlapping mental framework within the students' minds. For every event, we required an explanation for why it was being taught from the students' perspective. We didn't want it to be a generic explanation, so whenever possible we had instructors share their own stories about how they had used similar concepts in combat.

We also encouraged the students to speak up and ask why information was relevant when they weren't sure how it was applicable to them. While most of us have probably experienced situations where asking why was discouraged, that type of culture promotes compliance over understanding. We wanted fighter pilots who could think on their own.

The uncertainty of combat destroys even the best-laid plans, and for fighter pilots to thrive in combat, they needed to ask for explanations when their orders didn't make sense. Having the students ask why also provided feedback for the instructors to understand the weak points in their lessons, giving them an opportunity to strengthen them. It was a culture shift that ended up making a significant difference in the students' learning.

For every event, objectives were then established on how to achieve the why. The number of objectives depended on the event; however, we found that five was the optimum number—more than five often became too many things to keep track of, whereas fewer than five wasn't comprehensive enough. The objectives consisted of specific goals that could be graded afterward as either a success or failure. This ensured accountability and provided a starting point for the debrief once the event ended. Objectives that were specific and measurable were best; however, not every objective fit into that mold, which was okay—the goal was to optimize for the why, not for something that would be easy to grade. For the less specific objectives, the instructors needed to use their experience to make a judgment call. While on the surface this reduced standardization, it ultimately enabled a far more customized solution to be tailored to each student, resulting in a faster learning curve.

2. Make the training learner-centered

People come from a diverse set of backgrounds, and they all have a different understanding of how the world operates. After decades of learning and growing on their own, each person sees the world differently. For students to have an interconnected and overlapping mental model, an instructor must tie new concepts into the students' current understanding, not the other way around. Most people want to learn, and usually, it's a failure of the system when a student fails to grasp a concept. For our students, this meant customizing the training plan for each student and then updating it based on how the student was progressing. Many of our students were coming from a previous fighter aircraft, which meant they already had varying skill levels for the missions we were teaching. However, there was often negative transfer, meaning the skills they had learned in a previous fighter could, in some cases, be a detriment in the F-35. In these cases, more time needed to be spent to break these bad habits than for a less experienced pilot.

Our approach to teaching them was threefold: First, we created a custom syllabus based on their experience. This made sure we were focusing our limited resources on areas that would have the greatest effect. Next, we reduced class sizes so that the instructors could spend more time on each student's understanding of the concept being taught. Nothing is free in a resource-constrained environment, so we cut the total number of group events and instead relied on learning software for the more basic material. Finally, we grouped students together based on previous experience. Students who had flown the same type of aircraft often shared similar understanding, making it easier for the instructor to teach multiple students at once.

Many traditional methods fail to take into account that people aren't just passive receivers of knowledge but rather part of the learning experience itself. Instead of a lecture model, where instructors spoke at length, we wanted a conversational model that created a dynamic learning environment. We didn't need the students to parrot the textbook answers at the end of the course; we needed them to be able to apply the principles that were being taught while in combat. Memorization, therefore, was de-emphasized—it didn't push students to make new connections and solve problems in creative ways. Rote memorization is a convergent learning model that gears people toward finding one "right" answer. It runs counter to the real world, where there's rarely a single right answer but rather multiple good solutions with different costs and benefits that expand into vastly different second- and third-order effects. For example, in the past, pilots had what are referred to as *critical action procedures tests*, where they were required to handwrite important emergency procedures from memory. Such a high emphasis was placed on memorization that if a pilot misspelled a word or even misplaced punctuation, they would be grounded from flying. It was an outdated way of testing information retrieval—punctuation has no bearing on being able to perform the emergency action in the air. So, we got rid of those tests, along with dozens of other areas where memorization didn't serve a necessary and vital purpose. That meant eliminating long-standing traditions, such as memorizing the engine's operating limits, which, before digital readouts, were important to memorize. However, modern aircraft display information differently to pilots— flight computers will display the aircraft as green if everything is performing well, yellow if there's a minor issue, and red if there's a critical issue, along with the relevant information about the health of the aircraft. Instead of memorizing numbers, we needed the pilots to use their added mental bandwidth to ensure they were making the best decisions possible.

3. Coaching is more effective than evaluating

In many fields, instructors and teachers view themselves as gatekeepers rather than as facilitators of student learning. In the fighter community, we've found that if left unchecked, the system defaults to this behavior, which ultimately results in pilots who are less capable. Instead of viewing the training as an opportunity to weed out deficient pilots, we established the mentality that we were already working with talented students who could make it through the training. Our job wasn't to weed them out but to coach them throughout each training event so that they could leave as the best possible pilots.

Even though we were measuring the students on nearly every aspect of their training—some events had over one hundred parameters—it wasn't to fail them or reprimand them but simply to adapt their training going forward. Each student's training was dynamic based on how they were performing—a student who excelled in a particular phase could advance and skip similar training events while those struggling would be given additional repetitions. This allowed the students to focus on becoming the best possible fighter pilots instead of just trying to pass the training.

The key to establishing this mentality was to treat a failure by the student as a failure by the system. Anytime a student failed to meet expectations, they would be coached on ways they could do better next time. In addition, there would be an instructors-only debrief on what the system and instructors could have done better. While this step may sound simple, in execution it needs to be continually reinforced by strong leaders.

At the end of the day, we still needed to ensure the students were safe and capable pilots; however, that only represented a fraction of an instructor's job. We found that almost everything is coachable and correctable if identified early enough. Even supposedly intangible attributes, such as attitude, work ethic, and flying instinct, can be significantly improved if coached properly.

4. Continually assess where technology can augment your training

Technology is always progressing, continually opening opportunities to increase the effectiveness and efficiency of how we learn. What we've found is that virtual training can give us synthetic lessons that can be just as good as—or in some cases, even better than—an actual flight. For years, simulators have helped us bridge the gap between academic instruction and flying in the real aircraft. This was especially important for the F-35 training, because at the time, it cost nearly $50,000 an hour to operate, meaning we were limited in the number of flights we could use to train the students. The simulators we had were incredibly realistic—each one was the size of a two-story house, with a large domed room in the middle. In the center was an exact replica of the cockpit. High-end projectors were then used to display the artificial world onto the dome, creating a 360-degree view for the pilot. Even the $400,000 carbon fiber augmented reality helmets were the same as what we used in the actual jet. They were all linked together, allowing formations of aircraft to fight against artificial intelligence threats that could mimic real adversaries. The simulators we had represented the closest we could come to putting a student in an actual fighter aircraft. As one Air Force general said when he saw them for the first time, "These simulators are a monument to human engineering."

The downside was that simulators were extraordinarily expensive—in some cases more than the actual aircraft they were replicating. This meant only a few could be built, creating a secondary training bottleneck that was often worse than the real thing. Students would sometimes only have access to a simulator once per week, drastically slowing down their training. We realized that our pursuit for a hyperrealistic simulator had caused us to fall into the common trap of continuing to refine a matured technology without asking why it's necessary.

Back in the 1990s, these high-end simulators were needed because anything less didn't replicate flying well enough to be useful. However, computing power had progressed exponentially over the years, meaning that a 1990s-era simulator—which required a supercomputer to operate at the time—could now be run on a laptop. While there was still a place for these high-end simulators, for much of our training, it was overkill. And because simulator technology follows a power law—the law of diminishing returns—the cost of one high-end simulator could buy hundreds of lower-end devices to aid in the students' training. What we needed was a spectrum of devices that could each be used for different aspects of the training.

We started by issuing new students high-performance laptops along with a stick and throttle that replicated what's in the F-35. Of course, the laptops didn't come close to the high-end simulators, but they served a different purpose—students could use them for the simple things such as starting the aircraft, taxiing, and checklist training. The benefit was the students always had access to them. We even developed an unclassified flight model so that they could bring them home and practice in their free time.

Once each student had their own personal flight simulator, we began incorporating more of the classroom and textbook information into lessons built directly into the simulation. We developed software to turn it into a game with multiple levels, along with a virtual instructor to walk them through the maneuvers. This allowed them from the very beginning to merge concepts, experience, and information into one cohesive mental framework. For instance, when learning how to perform a takeoff, the simulator would pause and then zoom in to a cutaway of the engine and show the primary points where the engine could fail. It would then demonstrate what it would look like from the cockpit and how to run the associated checklists to safely recover the aircraft. It was a far more effective and integrated approach than the four-foot stack of paper that students had been given to memorize in the past.

Bridging the gap between the laptops and the high-end simulators were virtual reality systems to create an immersive flight environment. This allowed the students to practice maneuvers that required more finesse, such as flameout landings, which are difficult to replicate on a laptop screen. We also had instructors fly actual F-35 sorties with 360-degree cameras attached to the aircraft. These videos were then available to be viewed on virtual reality devices, giving the students examples of an experienced instructor performing the maneuver correctly. Overlays and text were then incorporated into the videos showing the instructor's cross-check and decision-making throughout each phase of the maneuver to further enhance the students' understanding.

Our spectrum-of-devices philosophy gave the students the opportunity to learn a new concept and practice it nearly simultaneously. The change in performance was so significant that we had to immediately begin rewriting the training syllabus so that we could continue to push the students. It carried over into other aspects as well. Instead of traditional lectures, we had students show up to the classrooms and learn on their laptops and virtual reality goggles while an instructor would be assigned to sit in and answer questions. This hybrid method allowed the students to learn how they wanted and at their own pace while allowing them to ask questions and engage in discussions that couldn't have been scripted ahead of time.

The use of technology to augment training needs to be continually reassessed. Technology often improves exponentially, which means that something that wasn't quite a good fit can quickly become useful. This isn't just for pilots—most career fields can benefit from enhanced data visualization, customized feedback, and synthetic training. Even for something as simple as rote memorization, performance can be significantly improved through software that customizes the training based on neuroscience coupled with feedback from previous training sessions.

5. Utilize an apprenticeship model

There are almost always people out there who already have a framework for how to succeed in a given field. To not utilize the mindset that these people have built over their careers is a tremendous waste of resources. In the fighter community, the best and most experienced pilots become instructor pilots. There isn't even an option for them to turn down the position. While we could easily find other instructors to teach the information, learning is more than just the information being taught—most of it is understanding how to organize and connect the information so that it becomes one cohesive framework. It's so important that we're willing to expend our most valuable resource on it.

To facilitate the students' understanding, the instructors would walk them through the way they would solve real-world tactical problems. This gave the students a chance to see how the instructors' mental framework operated. For even simple problems, the instructors were often pulling from many concepts at once—such as the physics behind their aircraft's mission systems, the psychology behind the enemy's mindset, the best practices behind air combat tactics, and how to balance risk and reward for different phases of the mission. This further reinforced to the students that actionable knowledge is built through interweaved concepts, not just memorizing information.

We found that two meetings before each flight worked best for developing the students' understanding. The first, called the *pre-brief,* consisted of an informal walkthrough of all the concepts that the training mission would be focusing on. The goal was to fill in any gaps in the students' understanding so that they had the necessary tools for the flight. The key to the pre-brief was the instructors asking the students open-ended questions about how they would solve different scenarios. Often, students thought they had a good understanding about a concept, but it wasn't until they had to use it in a scenario that their shortcomings became evident.

Once the students had demonstrated an understanding of a concept, we then introduced *heuristics.* When flying, time is of the essence, so anything we can do to shorten the amount of time it takes to make a decision is valuable. Heuristics are rule-of-thumb strategies designed to shorten the time it takes for people to solve complex problems—it allows people to function without constantly stopping to think about their next course of action. Heuristics are prioritization taken to the extreme where, given a specific set of conditions, you only have to cross-check a few things to solve highly complex problems. Though the concept may sound abstract, everyone uses them in their lives.

Take, for instance, a baseball player catching a ball. The math associated with calculating trajectories is complex, requiring differential equations to describe the forces acting on the ball. One solution would be for the player to solve those calculations and then run to the point where the calculations predicted the ball would be. That might be the most precise solution, but the time it takes to do that renders the method useless to the player. Instead, the player can look at the ball and freeze the angle while running toward it. By just doing those two things, the player will intercept the ball. Now, the heuristic doesn't ensure the player takes the optimum path, nor does it allow them, for instance, to run with their back to the ball for one hit over their head. However, it provides a shortcut that the player can use for a specific set of conditions.

It was this concept that was used during what became known as the "Miracle on the Hudson." An airliner taking off from LaGuardia Airport lost both its engines, and the pilots had to decide whether they could glide back to the airport or needed to find an alternate landing site. The copilot, Jeffrey Skiles, spotted the airport and noticed how it was moving across the windscreen. Here's what he said after the accident:

> It is not so much a mathematical calculation as visual, in that when you fly an airplane, a point that you can't reach will actually rise in your windshield. A point that you are going to overfly will descend in your windshield.

Because the airport was slowly moving up on the windshield as they flew toward it, he realized that they weren't going to make it. The captain, Sully Sullenberger, was therefore able to rule out the airport and instead chose to land on the Hudson River, saving all on board.

That concept—how an object tracks along the windscreen—is a heuristic that fighter pilots use all the time called *line of sight*. We're often trying to intercept other aircraft while putting ourselves in specific positions to employ our weapons. We don't have time to calculate the trajectories of the aircraft, so we use line of sight to understand how we're moving in relation to the other aircraft. We even have a simplified version for new students. For example, when the enemy turns, we'll have the students wait until the enemy's aircraft is lined up above their stick or throttle before following them. This allows them to maintain their range, allowing them to employ missiles while waiting for an optimal gun solution. On each training flight, they'll take a mental snapshot of the line of sight, and eventually, they'll transition to the more advanced heuristic that works throughout a wider range of applications.

The downside of heuristics, however, is that they only work under certain conditions. Because they're relying solely on a few key factors to make a decision, they're not as robust as fully understanding a concept. This often leads people to downplay their relevance. However, they should be seen as simply a tool that can aid in decision-making. For example, when planning missions, we'll have what we refer to as a *good-idea cutoff line*. During the mission-planning process, there are often hundreds of people working together to achieve an objective. It's natural and even desirable that everyone bring forth their best ideas for solving the various problems. However, before the planning even starts, the commander will set a time when the plan will be frozen—at that point, no new ideas will be accepted, and everyone will work to complete the current plan. Past experiences have shown that accepting new ideas after the good-idea cutoff line—which is usually set about two-thirds of the way through the planning process—often leads to delays and confusion and ultimately results in a lower mission-success rate. Of course, this is just a heuristic—if a great idea is brought forth toward the end of the planning process, or if there's something that hasn't been addressed that may lead to mission failure, the plan will likely be changed.

After the pre-brief the student would meet with their instructor several hours before the flight for a formal briefing. During the brief, the instructor would go over everything they expected to encounter during the mission along with the tactics they would be utilizing. The formal briefing served as a last look at the instructor's cognitive map while also setting expectations for the student. The student didn't need to solve the problems the same way as the instructor, but they needed to solve it in such a way as to keep their situational awareness high while also performing the tactic or maneuver safely. This gave the student the outer bounds for what was considered reasonable and ensured they were using best practices that had been proven to work. As the student's experience and skill set grew, these outer bounds were gradually expanded to allow the student to explore more of the envelope.

Whether it was in the simulator or in the air, the best learning occurred when both the student and the instructor had to work together to solve tactical problems. This created a dynamic environment that was messy and unpredictable, mimicking combat, where teamwork and communication are often more important than individual maneuvers. This pushed the student to extrapolate on concepts that were variations of the ones they had been taught, while those who had just memorized the solutions wouldn't be able to adapt to the changing conditions.

6. Set aside time to debrief

If you ask any fighter pilot what the most important part of learning is, without fail, they'll say the debrief. For our training missions, we'll fly for about an hour and a half, and then afterward, we'll spend several hours or, in some cases, several days debriefing the mission. Everything about the debrief is focused on how we can get better for the next flight. If something exceptionally good occurred, we'll point it out; otherwise, all our time is spent on what went wrong and how we can get better.

It often shocks new pilots how brutally honest our debriefs can be. After a full day of planning, briefing, and flying a mission, we'll gather in a room and spend hours picking apart everything that went wrong. These are the best pilots in the world, and even if all the objectives were met and the mission was a success, we'll still comb through the flight and find everything that can be improved.

Rank comes off in the debrief, meaning even the most senior officer or most experienced pilot is open to just as much criticism as the newest wingman. This is surprising to many who expect the military to follow a strict hierarchy. I've been in debriefs where a young flight lead has pointed out mistakes that the commander of the base made. The commander, instead of using his status as a shield, thanked the flight lead for pointing out his mistakes and talked through the ways he could improve for the next flight. That's the baseline expectation for any debrief.

A sortie almost never goes exactly according to plan: It's continually changing, forcing the pilot to make decisions in a harsh environment, often with limited information and time, not unlike in the business world. We're fighting a thinking adversary that's specifically targeting our weaknesses. We're in turn making decisions that are trying to exploit theirs— each side attempting to seize the initiative and, in the process, creating dozens of potential outcomes. In training, if the bomber we're escorting was shot down, or if an enemy aircraft bombed the point we were defending, it's usually multiple overlapping mistakes that led to the failure. Everyone likely had an opportunity at some point to intervene and save the mission. The fighter pilot debrief works because everyone is willing to take ownership of their mistakes.

Taking ownership is a difficult skill to master. Most people want to win and be seen in a positive light. In the debrief, though, with the mission already complete, the way to win is to accurately identify lessons that will make everyone better for the next mission. It's an unstable environment that only works when everyone is willing to first look inward for any failures. It only takes one person trying to pass the blame for the collaborative environment to fall apart. Because it's not stable, it requires constant maintenance, especially by those who could use their status to get by. The mission commander must be the first person to call themselves out, the pilot with the most experience must be willing to say they made a basic error, and the highest-ranking pilot must be willing to set the example to show that rank doesn't shield mistakes.

By treating everyone equally in the debrief, the mission can be analyzed in a sterile environment. We can figure out what went wrong and capture those lessons for future flights. To the casual observer, it's a brutal process, but to the pilots in the debrief, it's just a puzzle on how to get better.

The first phase of the fighter pilot debrief consists of data gathering. It's not uncommon to come back from a flight and have trouble remembering the details. When you're continuously focused on making split-second decisions, your brain doesn't have time to process everything that happened. I've flown in large exercises where I've been pushed to the limit, and just forty-five minutes after landing, my memory of the flight was hazy, like waking up from a dream.

With so many people participating in the debrief, it's critical that everyone has an accurate recollection of the mission before we begin to analyze it. Modern fighters record nearly every aspect of the jet from start-up to shutdown—all our screens are recorded, along with stick and throttle inputs, engine performance, flight control deflections, even what we're looking at. After landing, all this information is downloaded and processed so that we can individually replay the mission. We'll first watch through the replay on our own, taking notes at significant times, so that by the end, we'll have an exact understanding of our individual performance during the flight.

Once we've gathered the data from our own aircraft, the next phase is to reconstruct the entire mission. With so many people operating in different environments, such as the ground, air, space, and cyberspace, the reconstruction is where everyone's data is merged into a god's-eye-view of the mission and then projected onto large screens in the debriefing room. During the playback, participants will stop at significant events that occurred so that everyone has an accurate understanding of what happened. Speaking time is precious: With potentially hundreds of people in the room, there's no time for long-winded statements; only high-level information in a precise format is allowed. Throughout the reconstruction, an accurate model of what occurred during the mission will begin to take shape. The mission commander, along with their deputies, will look for failed objectives and take notes on potential reasons they may have occurred.

Once the reconstruction is over, the debrief will move into the analysis phase. Prioritization is key—the mission commander must identify the most important areas to focus on, which are called *debrief focus points*. These are failed objectives, such as friendly losses and high-level mistakes, that the group can learn from. The debrief will then transition to finding all the contributing factors that led to the mistake. These fall into three categories:

1. The first is that the person who made the mistake didn't **assess** the situation correctly. Their cross-check wasn't sufficient to build the necessary situational awareness before making the decision.

2. The second is that the person failed to **choose** the correct course of action. If the pilot chose the wrong tactic, then we'll look to understand why they made that decision and how they can change their decision-making criteria the next time they see a similar situation.

3. Finally, the pilot may have chosen the correct decision but **executed** it improperly. This often comes down to putting their jet, along with their wingman's jet, in the

correct location and then employing a valid weapon. Modern fighters are complex weapons systems that require many actuations in the correct sequence at the correct time.

The last part of the debrief is the instruction phase. This is where everything that was learned comes together and is then taught to all the participants. The mission commander will walk through the sequence of events that should have occurred given the new insights. They'll then tie the lessons into larger concepts and how they can be applied to real-world missions. The information is then recorded so that it can be reviewed prior to similar missions in the future.

Debriefing is one of the most powerful tools to improve decision-making. By understanding the cause and effect of the choices we make, we can build an understanding of the world around us. Most decisions are slight variations on ones we've already seen. The key is to, at a minimum, not make the same mistakes twice. Even better is to observe how others have successfully made similar decisions and incorporate their best practices into our learning process. This only works if you fundamentally understand the *why* and *how* behind the decisions—without that information, you're simply memorizing facts, which doesn't grow your understanding of how the world operates.

Over time, we can build an elaborate web of lessons that can account for a wide range of problems. By learning through concepts, we can make connections with seemingly unrelated topics to find creative solutions. Over time we're able to build a mental framework so that many decisions become automatic.

It's a mental tool kit that can rapidly recall past information to make future decisions.

But what about making a decision about a problem that you haven't encountered before? What happens when the variables are so complex that you're overwhelmed with the potential outcomes?

4

FAST-FORECASTING

Parwan Province, Afghanistan: 0200 Local Time

Looking out the front of my canopy, I could see a glow emanating from beyond the towering mountains ahead of me. My wingman, who went by the call sign Shark, and I were returning from a five-hour strike mission against a Taliban command-and-control center, followed by armed overwatch of a helicopter insertion. Even though we were over a hundred miles away from Bagram Air Base, the base's bright security lights were causing the dusty air to glow yellow high into the night.

Inside my cockpit, I finished writing down several notes about the mission that I wanted to pass to our intelligence analyst after we landed. I then began configuring my avionics for the approach, which is one of the most dangerous phases of flight. After a long mission in the middle of the night, it's easy to get complacent. Unfortunately, many pilots over the years have survived harrowing missions, only to crash on the flight home. At night and close to mountains, it only takes a moment of losing focus to turn a routine mission into a disaster.

The terrain in Afghanistan is particularly harsh—the mountains form the western edge of the Hindu Kush, which lead into the Himalayas and then Mount Everest. In certain parts of Afghanistan, the mountains are nearly *twenty-five thousand feet*—higher than the cruising altitude of many airliners. The extreme terrain makes all forms of aviation difficult. Even in the F-16, with one of the highest thrust-to-weight ratios of any aircraft, we had to plan our climbs so that we didn't get trapped in a valley. During the brief before our missions, we would often remind ourselves that should we have to eject over the mountains, we would need to manually separate from the seat; otherwise, we would impact the ground before the parachute deployed.

The high altitude also meant that we had to carry more speed when landing. Because the F-16 was designed to be the most maneuverable fighter in the world, the engineers stripped it of as much weight as possible. The brakes of the thirty-thousand-pound aircraft are similar in size to a Toyota Corolla's. When landing, you touch down at around 175 miles per hour and then aerobrake—balancing the nose of the aircraft in the air while the two main tires are on the ground. The wind resistance gradually slows the aircraft until you're at highway speeds; only then can you begin applying the brakes—any earlier will result in setting the brakes on fire. Bagram, though, was unique in that in addition to the high altitude, the runway only operated in one direction, which had a downward slope.

Our landing tonight would be more difficult than normal. We had been alerted that the primary runway was closed, leaving us with only the smaller runway—several thousand feet shorter and only half the width—to land on. Most of the base's traffic was during the day, so the night was when they could shut down a runway with minimal impact. My wingman and I were also both bringing back several thousand pounds of unexpended bombs. The added weight meant our approach speed would be faster than normal, putting even more stress on our brakes.

While having to land on the smaller runway was an inconvenience, this was a typical night in Afghanistan. Each mission, we had to adapt to changing conditions and find solutions to dozens of challenging problems. The primary concern, however, was that we didn't have a backup airfield in which to land. The international airport in Kabul was only thirty miles away and normally served as our divert airfield should Bagram shut down. However, they rarely coordinated with Bagram, and tonight, they too were closed, leaving our nearest divert airfield several hundred miles away.

This presented a problem. To land on the shorter runway, we would need to decrease our weight. However, we also wanted to keep enough fuel on board to land at a different airfield should something unforeseen happen. Tonight, it wasn't possible to do both. Because we were carrying some of the newest weapons in the Air Force inventory, we weren't authorized to dump them before landing. That meant the decrease in weight would have to come from our fuel.

If this had been a training mission, we would have aborted it due to the increase in risk. However, this was combat and there were lives at stake, particularly since we were the only aircraft that could provide armed overwatch during an important operation tonight. The increase in risk had been accepted by headquarters—we would carry extra fuel throughout the mission and then just prior to landing burn it off so that we could land on the shorter runway. This left a five-minute gap where we would be vulnerable.

As we approached Bagram, it was time to start burning off our excess fuel. Over the radio, I said, "One's gate," and engaged my afterburner. I could feel the jolt in thrust as my airspeed began increasing. I flipped up my night vision goggles in preparation for landing and could see my wingman keeping up with me as a thirty-foot white-and-blue flame flowed out the back of his aircraft. It was a quiet night, the radio was silent, and looking up, I could see hundreds of thousands of stars along with the distinct outline of the Milky Way—which, strangely, because of the lack of cultural lighting, looked brighter than the terrain beneath us. Cresting over the final fifteen-thousand-foot peak, Bagram came directly into view.

Bagram is better described as a sprawling armored city as opposed to just a base. At its peak, it was the home of over forty thousand military personnel and civilian contractors. First-time visitors were usually amazed that such a place could even exist—it looked like something out of a science fiction movie. For decades, nothing had been removed—as soon as something became obsolete, a replacement was built next to the original, giving it the appearance of a cluttered, high-tech landfill. From the air at night, the security lights could be clearly seen, drawing a sharp perimeter around the base, separating it from the dark, hostile countryside.

As I dove into the valley to prepare for landing, I checked in with the tower controller, who cleared us to land. With my wingman trailing behind me, we slowed down, lowered our gear, and began the final descent. I could hear the fatigue in my wingman's voice. Likely his "go pill" was wearing off—a specialized mix of dextroamphetamine developed by the military that we were issued before long missions. The pills acted as both a stimulant and a cognitive-performance enhancer, having been described as combining the best aspects of amphetamine and Adderall.

Suddenly, I began to see what looked like large, glowing, orange ropes climbing into the sky. My first thought was that sweat had run into my eyes and caused a flashing sensation. I blinked, expecting them to go away, but they were still there. It was such a strange sight that it took time for me to process what was going on. After what seemed like several seconds but in reality was probably far less, I realized that it wasn't sweat but that the base was under attack—the glowing ropes I was seeing were the base's defensive anti-mortar systems being activated.

Due to the continual attacks over the years, a series of Gatling cannons had been installed throughout the base to defend it from incoming projectiles. They were controlled by an automated system that detected incoming mortars and then shot the six-barrel cannons at them. Each shell, twenty-five times the size of a rifle bullet, was filled with high explosives that detonated near the mortar to destroy it. When we had first arrived at the base, we had been briefed on the system—a warning horn would sound just prior to it firing, and if we didn't cover our ears before it fired, the sound could rupture our eardrums. A few nights later, I had been walking to breakfast after a mission when one of the guns activated a few hundred feet away—the high-pitch spin-up of the barrels followed by the explosive roar of seventy-five rounds being shot each *second* caused such a deafening noise that you could feel it reverberate throughout your body while shaking your teeth.

Now I was seeing the system activate from the air. There were at least three cannons shooting from different parts of the base, creating a strange weaving pattern through the sky. The explosions from the self-destructing rounds were far larger than they appeared from the ground, giving the appearance of being inside a fireworks show. From my cockpit, the unfolding scene was silent, although it was quickly interrupted by the tower controller yelling that the runway had been hit and that we needed to immediately abort our landing.

Theoretically, the cannons should have been calibrated to prevent them from accidentally shooting us down; however, there had been several instances in the past where similar systems shot down friendly aircraft. With multiple cannons weaving tracer fire in front of us, I didn't want to take a chance.

Keeping your aircraft under control is always the most important task to focus on. My first concern was not hitting the ground. The tendency when slow and low to the ground is to pull back on the stick, causing the aircraft to stall and crash.

With that in mind, I slammed the throttle forward, selecting full afterburner, and raised my gear, while holding the aircraft level so that I could rapidly accelerate. Within seconds, I was back up to tactical maneuvering speed. I then pulled back on the stick, climbing vertically into the sky. Looking down, I saw another burst from the cannons as they attempted to engage another mortar volley. I flipped down my night vision goggles to see if I could find where the mortars were coming from; however, I only saw a sea of pixelated darkness.

As soon as my wingman and I got to a safe altitude, we took inventory of our jets. We were now well below our bingo fuel. The multiple compounding problems had led us down a dangerous path that was rapidly closing in on us. With the airfield still under attack and having already burned deep into our fuel reserves, the decisions we made in the next few minutes would be critical to our survival.

RISK

Decision-making, put simply, is betting on the outcome of a choice. When a lion hunts down a gazelle, it's intuitively calculating risk versus reward. Each attack expends large amounts of energy and comes with the potential for injury. To make the charge worth it, the lion needs to assess many factors and conclude that the reward is greater than the risk. In the case of a lion, because of their small hearts and lungs, stalking until they're close to their prey—usually within several dozen meters—is the most important factor. If it's unable to get close enough, it will wait for a better opportunity. As humans, we're continually making similar assessments of our environment. In many cases—particularly ones that we've encountered before—this intuitive assessment works well. However, with new or complex situations, we must move beyond our risk-versus-reward intuition and think in terms of expected value.

To find the expected value of a decision, we need to find the possible upside multiplied by the probability of it occurring, minus the downside multiplied by the probability of that occurring. By finding the difference, we can then see what the total benefit is. In its most basic form, say you have a bet of $1,000 with an 80 percent chance of winning and a 20 percent chance of losing. To find the upside, you multiply $1,000 by 80 percent (0.8), and get $800. The downside is $1,000 multiplied by 20 percent (0.2), which is $200. The difference between them is positive $600, making it a great bet to take. While this may seem obvious, many people struggle when there's a difference in the probability *and* outcome. Take another bet, only this time there's a 10 percent chance of winning $10,000 but a 70 percent chance of losing $1,000—should you take the bet? We can see that despite the odds of winning being much lower, the expected value is positive $300, meaning that it's still a good bet to take.

Of course, in the real world, it can be difficult, if not impossible, to determine the exact numbers to use. This is called the *base of sand problem* and plagues computer models—despite how elaborate and sophisticated the model is, it's often impossible to precisely forecast the future. The solution, therefore, is to forgo the illusion of precision and use a technique called *fast-forecasting.*

Fast-forecasting relies on extrapolating our intuition to

approximate the expected value of a decision. This is why concepts are so important to learn. Whereas facts only represent individual data points, concepts encompass entire regions of understanding. By understanding many adjacent concepts, we can build a broad tapestry of understanding that enables us to quickly approximate a ballpark solution. This allows us to combine the best aspects of our instincts with the best aspects of modeling.

In fast-forecasting, we are, in effect, building a mental model of the problem. Because our minds can only balance a fraction of the information that a computer can, this overcomes our natural inclination to include as many variables and data as possible. We're forced to simplify. In almost every system, there are only a few variables that, due to strong power laws, drive the system—those are the ones to focus on. For instance, when it comes to ejecting from an aircraft, more than anything else, slowing down is the single most important factor for survival. That's because wind resistance doesn't affect the force linearly but exponentially. Think of sticking your hand outside of a car going sixty miles per hour—now imagine that force at six hundred miles per hour. Because speed has an exponential impact on the wind resistance, instead of ten times the force, it's actually one hundred times the force, meaning that your hand would likely be ripped off. As a pilot, that means that although there are a dozen steps to carry out before ejecting, just slowing down is far more important than everything else combined.

Likewise, when it comes to investing, compound interest—where the interest you're receiving from an investment is immediately reinvested—is an extraordinarily powerful force and the single most important concept for a typical investor to understand. However, many people instead tend to focus on maximizing their interest rate. Because economies are relatively efficient, any investment that promises to outperform the stock market often carries an increase in risk unless the investor has specific knowledge that's not available to the public. Therefore, by identifying time as the most important variable to wealth, a typical investor can find a *good enough* investment, and begin investing in it as soon as possible. For example, if thirty years ago you had invested $1,000 in the S&P 500—a fund that simply tracks the top five hundred companies in the United States—while continuing to invest $200 into it each month, you would currently have over $400,000, despite having only put in $72,000. However, if you had instead waited until ten years ago to invest, you would've needed to have found an investment that could sustain a near 30 percent interest rate to make a similar amount of money. That investment—again, because markets are relatively efficient—would've likely carried a very high risk both in terms of underperformance as well as a devastating loss of all money, making the expected value far less than the first investment.

The key to fast-forecasting is to not get overwhelmed by the details—logic and reason are what drive the technique. Precision is often the enemy of conceptual thinking. What we're trying to do is bring to bear the mental framework that we've accumulated over our lifetimes to estimate the expected value of a decision. If we instead make the problem overly complex, we lose the ability to quickly manipulate the relevant information through the lens of our concepts, principles, heuristics, and facts.

As fighter pilots, one of the sayings we have is that no decision *is* a decision, and it's usually the worst one to make. On each mission, we're bombarded with thousands of decisions, forcing us to prioritize and then make decisions as quickly as possible. While flying a fighter is physically demanding—often causing us to lose upward of five to ten pounds of water weight each flight—the mental aspect is far more difficult. Throughout a flight, my brain feels like it's in overdrive as I jump from decision to decision, rarely thinking about anything that's not relevant to the sortie. After a complex mission, my thoughts feel scrambled, usually taking a full day to mentally recover. The flights are so demanding and the consequences so high that before a mission, the Air Force legally requires us to go into twelve hours of crew rest where we can't be distracted with any work-related events.

Although life outside the cockpit is usually not as intense, speed is still critical. Most of us have more tasks to do than we're capable of doing, meaning time is an important resource that we must use to our advantage. In addition, because mental capacity is a finite resource, there's only so much thinking we can do in a given amount of time before mental fatigue begins to cloud our judgment. Therefore, each minute we *don't* make a decision needs to be factored in as a cost that we're incurring. This cost should be subtracted from the value of waiting to gain additional information. Because gaining more information often follows the law of diminishing returns, we will at some point cross the threshold where we're losing value by continuing to delay a decision. It also means that, despite how hard we try, we'll never have a perfect understanding of a system. Although humans crave certainty, all decisions come with uncertainty and risk.

For decisions that can be changed, it's often best to decide early and adjust them as more information is learned. This can have the effect of resetting the diminishing-gain curve, which allows for a better assessment given the same amount of time and effort. This technique of *failing fast* and iterating can be very effective for small teams and for new fields that carry a high amount of uncertainty. On the other end of the spectrum, if the decision is important and irreversible, it makes sense to spend additional time gathering more information before choosing a course of action. However, even for those decisions, speed is still necessary to quickly eliminate nonviable options so that the weight of effort can be better focused on the remaining options.

For many, mental arithmetic is the most difficult part of fast-forecasting—if that's the case, you're not simplifying enough. It's always better to oversimplify than under-simplify when fast-forecasting, so make it simple—you can always refine your solution later. Don't think of this as a final solution but rather the first of several steps. We're starting with the big-picture concept and slowly adding in detail until we have a good enough resolution to make the decision. Some decisions are obvious early on while others will require more refinement. This allows us to be agile, quickly running through different scenarios and understanding their implications before choosing the correct action.

Even complex formulas can often be mentally solved by

utilizing nontraditional methods that take advantage of how our brains function. Take the conversion from Fahrenheit to Celsius, a nonlinear relationship that most people have trouble mentally calculating. Here's the equation:

$$°C = 5/9(°F—32)$$

However, instead of calculating the formula or looking it up, both actions that pause our thinking and provide friction toward seeing the big picture, we can take a different approach that visually approximates the solution. Take a look at the following numbers—they're inverted or have some other mental hook that makes them easy to remember:

$$-40°F = -40°C$$
$$41°F = 4°C$$
$$61°F = 16°C$$
$$82°F = 28°C$$
$$104°F = 41°C$$

I imagine a physical number line, like a long ruler. Whenever I need to convert between the two, I'll just extrapolate off the memorized numbers. If the temperature is, say, 70°F, I'll roughly take the difference between the memorized numbers. In this case, it's 22°C, which turns out to be within one degree of the actual answer. By utilizing this technique, I can always roughly convert between Celsius and Fahrenheit without having to distract myself to look it up or calculate it.

Extrapolating off memorized numbers is a technique called *staking* and is used throughout nearly every aspect of flying fighters to speed up our decision-making. Many of our tactics are reliant on calculating the relationship between multiple moving bodies over time. Whether it's dog-fighting against another aircraft or geolocating an enemy surface-to-air missile system, calculus is often required to precisely solve the tactical problem. There isn't time to do differential equations in the air; however, we don't need to—it's been solved ahead of time, and we just need to extrapolate off a few key numbers. This concept is used for everything from our fuel management, weapons timing, and missile fly-outs to managing our stealth attributes, and many other complex decisions. It's also used outside the cockpit—when we're planning large missions often there are hundreds of moving parts that need to be allocated and sequenced to give us the best possible chance of achieving our objectives. By roughly fast-forecasting the expected value of different tactics, we can gradually home in on the best solution.

Fast-forecasting isn't tied to air combat—any field can take advantage of the technique. Fast-forecasting allows people to quickly generate a rough solution that logically makes sense. In some cases, the expected value of alternatives may be so different that the best solution is obvious and any additional time and bandwidth can be spent on the next decision. In others, it can quickly narrow down the alternatives so that further analysis can be focused only on what's viable, saving time and resources.

The real world is complex, and decisions always come with some amount of uncertainty. Fast-forecasting is effective in this environment because it prioritizes accuracy over precision by integrating our hard-earned intuition into the solution. In team settings, this means there may be debates about the correct decisions to make. If that's the case, the first step is to analyze how each party is generally looking at the problem. Numbers are always secondary to concepts, so logic and reason should be used to find the best methodology for solving the problem. Once that's accomplished, it will significantly narrow down the options to choose from. Only then should we turn our focus to the numbers being inputted.

If this sounds messy, it's because it is. Finding the precise probability outside of dice rolls and coin flips is difficult, if not impossible, for most systems. Combined with most people having an intense aversion to uncertainty, this often leads them to seek answers outside of their own logic, whether it's through committees or computer models. However, by thinking critically and embracing uncertainty, we can come up with better decisions. This isn't to say that every decision will be perfect, but at a minimum we can eliminate the bad options, giving us a much higher probability of success over time.

AFGHANISTAN: 0230 LOCAL TIME

For the last minute, the radio had been erupting in chatter. Now, with the attack over, it was silent as everyone took inventory of their situation. In my formation, we were both almost out of fuel and didn't have a viable place to land—one of the worst places to be as a pilot.

Aviation accidents usually consist of many improbable events that all occur consecutively to bypass the redundancies that have been put in place to prevent such occurrences. In this case, the mortar attacks had unfortunately occurred during the small window when we were most vulnerable. If they had been five minutes prior, we would have been able to divert to Mazar-i-Sharif air base, located several hundred miles to the north. If they had occurred five minutes later, we would have been safely parked in a fortified revetment. However, we were now above the damaged base with minimal fuel and few remaining options. Calculating my fuel burn rate, I realized that we had about fifteen minutes of fuel before we flamed out.

The first option was landing on the damaged runway. The control tower told us that the status of the damage was unknown—they wouldn't be able to send someone out to assess the damage until the base's explosive ordnance disposal team cleared the area of all unexploded munitions. All they could tell us was that they had seen a mortar shell impact near the middle of the runway, but they couldn't see the extent of the damage from their location. They estimated the runway would be closed for at least the next thirty minutes.

Even though the runway was closed, we still had the option of attempting a landing on it. Mortar shells are relatively small, and even though one had destroyed our squadron's truck a few weeks prior, they would likely just create large potholes in the concrete runway. The chances of us hitting one were low; however, at night, they would be impossible to avoid. If we did hit one, it could quickly cartwheel the jet before we had time to eject, almost certainly resulting in a fatality.

The alternative was to wait and hope the runway opened

before we ran out of fuel. If it didn't, we could eject from our aircraft. Although the ACES II ejection seat in the F-16 is reliable, it's not perfect. Dozens of complex sequences need to occur in quick succession to explosively separate the pilot from the aircraft and parachute them to the ground. If you're riding the "silk elevator," as pilots call it, there's no redundancy if it fails. There's also a significant chance of injury from the crushing force of the rocket motor igniting, often breaking a pilot's neck and back. In addition, when flying in a combat zone, there's also an enemy that's trying to hunt you down and needs to be factored into any decisions.

Neither option was ideal, but I needed a worst-case plan before I looked into more creative solutions. I used fast-forecasting to find the expected value of each option. At this point, there was no upside, so I just had to look at the downsides. If we landed on the damaged runway and one of us hit a crater, we could destroy the plane and, much more importantly, kill ourselves. This was a high potential downside; however, there's a difference between possibility and probability. To find the expected value, I needed to know the probability of it happening. Because I didn't have much information to go on and time was running out, there would be a high amount of uncertainty. Still, it was the best I could do given the situation.

The runway, I knew, was seventy-five feet across, which I rounded to one hundred feet. One to two mortar shells had hit the runway, each of which I assumed caused a one-foot crater. Based on my landing roll, that meant a little more than 2 percent of the runway was affected. If any one of my three tires hit a damaged portion of the runway, it could result in the jet cartwheeling. Multiplying the two together, this gave a 6 percent chance of hitting a crater. However, just because a wheel hit a crater didn't necessarily mean the jet would cartwheel—I guessed there was about a 50 percent chance of that occurring. Therefore, with a high amount of uncertainty, I estimated a 97 percent survival rate for each of us. While I had made many assumptions—some likely flat-out wrong—it was the best I could do given the circumstances. Even if I was off by a factor of two, it gave me confidence that the situation was manageable without having to resort to an extreme course of action.

Next, I began calculating the expected value of ejecting. The United States has lost over *six hundred* F-16s since they went into service, so there's a large amount of data on the ejection seat. While many pilots have died ejecting, most of them were outside of the ejection envelope—they ejected too late, too fast, or too low. However, for those who ejected within the envelope, there's only been a handful of times that the seat has malfunctioned, making the ACES II one of the most reliable ejection seats in the world. Based on the data, I estimated there was a 98 percent chance of surviving the ejection, on par with landing on the damaged runway. However, there was also a high chance of a significant injury—greater than 50 percent—and a 100 percent chance of losing the aircraft. In addition, if we didn't eject directly over the base, there was a chance that we could be captured or killed by the enemy. At this point, I didn't need to total up the downsides; it was clearly not as good of an option as landing on the damaged runway, and therefore, I eliminated it.

The whole process up to this point had taken about fifteen

seconds. I now had reason and logic that landing on the damaged runway was the better option. I also understood that the situation sounded worse than it actually was—even though the runway was closed, it was not as though it had been completely destroyed. With that, I told the tower controller that we would likely be landing on the damaged runway in ten minutes—that would give us time to try to find a better solution while also giving each of us two attempts at landing, a good trade-off between maximizing our time and building in redundancy. The controller replied that he couldn't authorize us to land on a damaged runway, only that we could land at our own risk. The hidden meaning was that we would be going against regulations and that I would bear any consequences if something went wrong.

Now that I had an acceptable plan that would likely ensure our survival, I turned my attention to finding a better one. One of the options that crossed my mind was a maximum-range maneuver called a *sky hook,* where we climbed to a very high altitude, into the stratosphere, to increase our efficiency and range. This could allow us to potentially reach Mazar-i-Sharif air base. However, running the math, I calculated that we would likely flame out before we got there. If absolutely necessary, we could still probably glide our jets into the airfield; however, it was clearly an inferior option to landing on the damaged runway and therefore quickly eliminated.

We were running out of time, but there were still two other potential options. The first was seeing if there was an airborne tanker that could meet us in the next few minutes. They often entered the country early and would set up holding patterns while they waited for aircraft to refuel from them. I didn't know where the next mission was taking place, but if it was close by, then we'd have a shot at refueling. The second option was seeing if the construction work at Kabul International Airport had finished early for the night. If they were done, then potentially, the runway would be usable even though it was still technically closed. I told the tower controller to call up Kabul and check on the status of the runway while I looked into finding the nearest tanker. Switching my radio to satcom, I keyed the mic to contact headquarters, who went by the call sign Trinity.

> HASARD: Trinity, this is Viper 51. Where's the nearest tanker? We're emergency fuel, and Bagram's shut down.
> TRINITY: Viper 51, the nearest tanker, call sign Mojo, is seventy-five miles to the east and entering their holding pattern for Viper 61 flight.
> HASARD: Copy, we're going to try to use them. What frequency are they on?
> TRINITY: Mojo is on Blue 47.

Even though all satellite communications were encrypted, we still used code words for the frequencies. Flipping through my book of frequencies, I found Blue 47 and entered the specific frequency into my radio.

> HASARD: Mojo, Viper 51—we're over Bagram and are emergency fuel. I need you to fly at max speed toward Bagram ASAP.
> MOJO: Viper, we can be there in about ten minutes.

By this point, we had seven minutes until our self-imposed landing time. The tanker was a promising option but one that could give us false hope and lead us to running out of fuel. Now that it was flying toward us at their max speed, I radioed the tower controller about the status of Kabul airport. He said that the construction was finishing up for the night. There were still people and equipment on the runway, but they could potentially clear it in the next few minutes. Based on previous experience, anytime someone uses the word *potentially*, they're trying to help, but are really just guessing. I told my wingman we were skipping Kabul. We now had two options: land on the damaged runway or refuel from the tanker.

We didn't have time to wait for the tanker to come to us. If we wanted to refuel, then we would have to fly away from the airfield and intercept it. The risk was that if anything failed while trying to refuel, we wouldn't be able to make it back to Bagram. Again, rough mental math enabled us to break down the problem.

The tanker was about eighty miles away and likely flying about 0.8 times the speed of sound—about eight miles per minute—meaning they would get overhead in ten minutes. If we flew toward them at a similar speed, we could rejoin in five minutes; however, we wouldn't have enough fuel to make it back to Bagram if something went wrong and we couldn't refuel. Based on previous experience, I estimated the chance of both of us being able to refuel at about 95 percent, on par with landing on the damaged runway. The upside was that if it worked, it would eliminate our problem since we'd have enough fuel to divert or wait until the runway was fixed.

However, the downside was that if anything failed, we would be forced to eject away from our base and above the fifteen-thousand-foot terrain that was scattered with ISIS and Taliban fighters. With that downside, it was probably better to go with the simpler option and just land without attempting to refuel. However, there was potentially a third option.

By intercepting the tanker at a slower airspeed, we could, instead of meeting in the middle, only travel one-third of the way while the tanker traveled two-thirds. This would allow us to save fuel while also keeping us closer to the base. If we couldn't refuel, then we would have just enough fuel to make it back to Bagram. This hybrid option gave us one shot at refueling while also preserving the fail-safe option of landing. The margins were razor-thin, though. Once we hit our bingo time, even if we were within arm's reach of the tanker, we would need to abort. We would also have only enough fuel for one landing attempt.

I told my wingman that we were going to try to refuel. I then gradually turned toward the tanker, being careful to not bleed off any airspeed, which would require pushing up the throttle and result in burning more fuel. As we continued the turn, the bright lights of the base fell away, and the dark silhouettes of the mountains came into view. The thought crossed my mind that I hoped this worked and that our fuel gauges were accurate, because ejecting above these mountains likely wasn't survivable. Even if the search-and-rescue helicopters knew where we were, they wouldn't be able to climb high enough into the thin air to come rescue us.

At this point, there wasn't much we could do. I rechecked

the math and called for a fuel check from my wingman. He was several hundred pounds lower than I was. After nearly a minute, I began to see a radar return slowly start marching down my display. I placed my cursor over it and locked it up, which began to show me the data I would need to complete the rejoin in my green heads-up display. Under my night vision goggles, I could also see the tanker's faint infrared strobe light flashing, distinguishing it from the hundreds of stars surrounding it.

Rejoining with the tanker is always a balancing act. If you're too aggressive with your intercept, you'll overshoot its flight path, which runs the risk of a collision. If you're too conservative, you can get stuck several miles behind the tanker, wasting precious fuel and time trying to catch back up. Tonight, the rejoin would have to be nearly perfect; otherwise, we might as well abort and head directly back to base to land.

Eventually, the tanker came into sight. I slowly pushed the throttle forward while rechecking my fuel and our range to the base. We only had about two minutes before we had to abort the attempt. To conserve fuel, my wingman stayed closer than normal, mimicking every throttle change that I applied. Over the radio, I told the tanker I was visual and was given clearance for the rejoin.

For all the chaos that had occurred over the last ten minutes, this was something that I knew I could control. Having done the maneuver hundreds of times before, I had confidence that I could make it happen. As soon as the tanker started tracking along my canopy, I rolled into it and pulled back on the stick. Because I was trying to save fuel and was slower than normal, I had to be more aggressive with the cut-off angle. I was now pointed in front of the tanker on a collision course. As the size of the tanker began to fill up my field of view through my night vision goggles, I slowly pulled my power back while drifting aft of the tanker, ending with us rolling out right behind it.

Over the radio, I told my wingman, "Pre-refueling checks, you're going first." He was lower on fuel, but more importantly, I wanted to put him in the easier position. If there was any delay, he could use my time to refuel while I split off and landed on the damaged runway. The urge to tell him to nail the refueling came over me, but I chose to remain silent—he knew the stakes, and any extra stress was likely to decrease his performance.

I pulled my power back and drifted to the side of the tanker. As I flipped up my night vision goggles, I could see the long boom extending behind the tanker with a small light at the end. Ahead, I could see the bright lights of Bagram as we got closer to the airfield. Over the radio, the boom operator cleared my wingman for contact. Slowly, he moved forward as I watched the boom swing out of his way. He then stabilized under the tanker, mildly rocking from the turbulence generated by the tanker's inboard engines. After several seconds, the boom extended, and the operator called "Contact" over the radio. Fuel was now flowing into his nearly empty tanks. After a minute, with several thousand pounds of fuel transferred, he disconnected so that I could get a few sips of fuel before he went back on.

As he pulled to the side of the tanker, I dropped behind

the boom and heard, "Cleared contact." I bumped up my throttle and started inching toward the tanker. We were now almost directly over the base, which was my cue to abort the refueling. Looking at the director lights underneath the plane, I could see a flashing *F*, telling me to go forward. Despite our technical advancement and technology, refueling is still 100 percent a manual maneuver. As my canopy neared the boom, it slowly swung to my right so close that I could have touched it if the canopy weren't there. Even though we were both traveling nearly 350 miles per hour, everything appeared stationary, as if I were slowly walking behind a parked airliner. Eventually, the light stopped flashing. Mentally, I took a snapshot of the giant silhouette of the tanker above me and froze the dimensions so that I didn't drift up or down. Seconds later, I felt a jolt as the boom plugged into my aircraft. I was now docked to the tanker and could feel the boom moving my aircraft around. After several seconds of holding my position while looking at the director lights and occasionally glancing down at the small fuel gauge by my right knee, I finally began to see it tick up. Fuel was now pouring into my aircraft. After a minute, I disconnected so that my wingman could continue refueling.

On the ground, the explosive ordnance team was able to clear the runway so that the airfield maintenance team could assess the damage. It turned out there was a crater on the runway, which they were able to patch. It's difficult to tell whether we would have hit it or not. Fortunately, we didn't have to test it. After another round of refueling from the tanker, we were both able to eventually land, bringing a close to the mission.

HUMANS AS DECISION-MAKERS

Over the course of a second, nearly twenty trillion impulses of information course through the neurons in our brains. By comparison, it takes a modern supercomputer forty minutes to replicate just *one second* of brain activity. Our brains merge memory and processing together into an extraordinarily effective package. What can take computers millions of steps to calculate can often be done in just a few hundred neuron transmissions. And through neuroplasticity, our brains can quickly rewire themselves, adapting to new and changing conditions. Amazingly, this is all done on just twenty watts of power.

Because computers rely on statistical regressions to look at past data and find correlations, they fail miserably at anticipating when a pattern will change—something humans are great at, because we seek to find causation, not just correlation. Once an environment changes, humans far outstrip computers in their ability to adapt. Nothing comes close to the way our minds can connect one pattern to a seemingly unrelated different pattern, forming the basis for creativity.

This is one of the reasons why humans are so adept at solving complex problems that often bog down computers. We're far more efficient and creative at developing an understanding of the system we're observing. We don't have to crunch every number to make a decision. We can use simple tools to understand complex relationships. Take, for instance, a basic graph—by translating raw numbers into a visual representation, we can take advantage of the brain's extremely fast and efficient visual cortex. It's a common saying that a picture's worth a thousand words; however, depending on the picture, it can be worth far more. As fighter pilots, we've translated nearly every important relationship in combat aviation into some form of data visualization. This started in the 1970s, when Colonel John Boyd developed the energy-maneuverability diagram by graphing an aircraft's turn rate versus its airspeed. By making this diagram for each aircraft in the world, pilots were able to overlay their aircraft's diagram with the enemy's and quickly see the conditions where they held an advantage and a disadvantage.

Humans are great at making decisions because of our ability to make sense of things—to weave a lifetime of knowledge in dozens of fields across thousands of experiences into an overlapping model of understanding. We can think conceptually, critically, metaphorically, and imaginatively. We think with common sense, which even the most sophisticated artificial intelligence programs lack.

However, when we rashly turn over our decision-making to external aids, such as committees or computers, we lose the ability to bring the full power of our brain to bear on a problem. We, in essence, have carved out a hole in our understanding and replaced it with someone else's solution. If we don't learn the underlying concepts behind that new information, then we're blindly trusting that it's correct. We lose the ability to quickly reconfigure concepts into creative solutions, which is one of the great strengths of the human mind.

This isn't to say that we shouldn't collaborate. There's far too much information in the world for one person to know it all. Also, diversity of thought is important—someone may have found a better way of looking at the problem. However, the person making the decision should roughly understand every concept involved and why the expected value leads toward the decision being made. If they don't, they should continue to ask *why* until they possess that understanding.

Credibility is an important element to account for when collaborating on a solution. The more competent someone is in a given field, the more they should trust their own intuition and understanding. The same holds true for a computer model—if the results have been validated successfully many times over, then it should be seen as a credible source. However, in both cases, a well-reasoned argument should supersede any perceived credibility.

One of the best tools to ensure we're thinking critically and not blindly handing off our decision-making is to fast-forecast a solution on our own. When we're forced, on the spot, to estimate the expected value of a decision, there's nowhere to hide. We can't push off the decision to someone else or a computer. We must use the concepts, principles, heuristics, and information that we've learned over our lifetimes to arrive at a solution. If someone or something else arrives at a different answer, then we can use logic and reason to figure out why and who is more likely to be correct. As a leader, this can be one of the most effective tools for preventing groupthink and for facilitating critical thinking. By having each person involved in the decision-making process formulate their own fast-forecast before hearing other solutions, people are forced to have conviction and stand behind their thought process.

Although our brains have evolved to be highly adept at cost-benefit decisions, they can be greatly improved by applying the principles of probability through fast-forecasting. Even for complex high-level thinking, this approach can be beneficial. Take theoretical physics, which would seem to be so complex and so precise that an approximate approach wouldn't be of much value. However, here's a quote by Richard Feynman, one of the top physicists of the twentieth century:

> I spent a few years trying to invent mathematical things that would permit me to solve the equations, but I didn't get anywhere, and then I decided that in order to do that I must first understand more or less how the answer probably looks. It's hard to explain this very well, but I had to get a qualitative idea of how the phenomenon works before I could get a good quantitative idea. In other words, people didn't even understand roughly how it worked, and so I have been working . . . on understanding roughly how it works, not quantitatively yet, with the hope that in the future that rough understanding can be refined into a precise mathematical tool.

No matter how difficult a decision is, you can, on your own, come up with the expected value of it. It's a starting point that holds you accountable for understanding the relationships within a system. It can always be later adapted and refined. However, fast-forecasting a solution prevents us from giving up our most valuable resource: the ability to think critically.

Up to this point, we've looked at how to choose the best option based on its expected value. The question is, though: How can we develop more options, particularly nontraditional ones that have the power to be a more effective solution?

5

CREATIVITY

On the afternoon of January 16, 1991, a dusty rental car sped across the tarmac at the Al Jouf forward operating base in eastern Saudi Arabia. Located along the Iraqi border, the desolate outpost had been selected as the launch point for the opening salvo of the Gulf War. In the car was the commanding officer of the base, who had just received a top-secret message that after months of planning and countless hours of rehearsals, their mission was a go—in just under twelve hours, his crews would be taking off, signaling the beginning of a massive, coordinated attack against the regime of Saddam Hussein.

The success of their mission was vital to the war—they would be tearing a hole in the Iraqi air defense network, which would allow coalition fighters to slip through under the element of surprise and strike critical targets throughout the country. The mission was so important that both the

Chairman of the Joint Chiefs of Staff and the Secretary of Defense had personally flown to Saudi Arabia to review their plans.

The lead-up to the attack had started six months earlier when Saddam Hussein, unable to repay the billions of dollars he had borrowed from Kuwait to finance his war with Iran, had invaded the small, oil-rich country. Within hours, it fell, and soon thereafter, he renamed it as Iraq's nineteenth province. Further destabilizing the region, the Iraqi dictator began mobilizing his military for an invasion of Saudi Arabia, which, if successful, would give him control of over half of the world's known oil reserves.

The international community reacted with fear and outrage. Initially, the response was confined to diplomatic channels—both the UN Security Council and the Arab League condemned the invasion and called for an immediate withdrawal of Iraqi forces. Soon thereafter, economic sanctions were placed on Iraq along with a naval blockade to impose a full trade embargo.

With Saddam continuing to threaten Saudi Arabia, President George H. W. Bush, at the request of Saudi Arabia's King Fahd, launched Operation Desert Shield to protect the country, dispatching two naval battle groups along with hundreds of U.S. Air Force F-15s and F-16s for around-the-clock air patrols. Simultaneously, he authorized the commanding officer of the coalition's forces, General Norman Schwarzkopf Jr., to begin planning for an offensive operation to remove Saddam's forces from Kuwait in the event diplomatic and economic means failed.

The planning for the air war took place in the basement of a Royal Saudi Air Force building in Riyadh that was nicknamed the "Black Hole," as those who were selected and sent past the armed guards never seemed to reemerge. Only those inside the bunker knew that the true purpose of them being there was for an offensive attack. To those outside—even to their supervisors—the nature of their mission was purely defensive. This meant that many of the planners had to juggle a separate cover job so that they didn't arouse suspicion. It was there that the planners worked out the basics of a four-phased strategic air campaign, including a critical first strike to destroy the early-warning radar sites located in western Iraq, effectively blinding Saddam.

At the time, Iraq's army was the fourth largest in the world, with over a million soldiers who were equipped with a substantial inventory of technologically sophisticated weapons—including a multilayered air defense system with over *seven hundred* tactical aircraft and *sixteen thousand* surface-to-air missiles. Utilizing Soviet doctrine, their air defense was designed around a computerized system called KARI, which served as an automated command-and-control system that turned the disparate units into one cohesive fighting force that Saddam could control. The KARI system was housed in an underground bunker just outside of Baghdad, which was now the most heavily defended point in the world. Protected by nearly 65 percent of Iraq's surface-to-air missiles and over half of its antiaircraft artillery, it was several times more defended than Hanoi during the Vietnam War, which was at the time considered among the most heavily defended places on the planet.

Destroying the KARI system was identified by the planners as one of the top priorities for the opening strikes of the war. The Iraqis relied on KARI almost to a fault, and destroying it would leave many of the units without guidance and unable to mount a coordinated defense. However, because it was such a hardened target located deep within enemy territory, striking it outright wasn't possible without first fighting into the country.

Feeding information into the KARI system was a chain of early-warning radar sites on the outskirts of the country that served as its eyes. As soon as coalition aircraft entered Iraq's airspace, they would be detected, leaving ample time for Saddam to raise his air defenses and potentially launch a counterattack with his tactical missiles, some of which were thought to be filled with chemical weapons. What was needed was a covert way to destroy a few of the radar sites to create a corridor so that the hundreds of coalition fighters could fly into the country undetected and strike vital targets, to include the KARI system and even Saddam himself.

The Iraqi air defense system had been designed primarily for defending the country from Iran to the east, Syria to the north, and Israel to the west. However, the country hadn't anticipated an attack from its southern border along Saudi Arabia. That meant the coalition forces massing in Saudi Arabia only needed to break through a "picket fence" of early-warning sites instead of the formidable overlapping coverage around the rest of the country. With help from the CIA and an engineer who had helped design the KARI system, planners were able to identify three radar sides that, if destroyed, would create a twenty-mile-wide corridor for the air assault to fly through.

The problem, however, was finding a way to attack the radar sites covertly. If any of the radars detected an attack, they would immediately pass the information along to the KARI system, and the entire Iraqi air defenses would be raised. This ruled out a conventional strike by fighters or bombers, who would be detected as soon as they crossed the border into Iraq. Even flying at low altitude, they would be seen with enough time for the radar sites to get the word out that an attack was underway.

Another problem facing the planners was ensuring destruction of the sites. The Iraqis were constantly moving their equipment around, making themselves difficult to target. With intelligence often several days old, this meant that any attacking force had to be prepared to be flexible and adjust their aim points once they had visually acquired the targets. This ruled out the possibility of a cruise missile and Tomahawk strike. Also, the missiles wouldn't be able to pass a battle-damage assessment after the strike, which would be crucial information for the follow-on aircraft.

As the planners continued to look for a solution, one of them happened to walk by a young captain named Randy O'Boyle. O'Boyle flew the lumbering MH-53 Pave Low helicopter and had been assigned to help develop the air war's search-and-rescue plans for pilots that were shot down behind enemy lines. O'Boyle was looking at a map of the country with all the enemy units drawn on it. As the planner walked by, O'Boyle was explaining to another pilot how his helicopters could destroy several of the sites, allowing them to push farther into the country and reduce the time it took them to rescue downed pilots. The planner asked how he intended to destroy the sites, to which O'Boyle, whose unit had been working extensively with counterterrorism units before the war, said that special forces teams could infiltrate into the country on the ground, destroy the sites, and then be picked up by Pave Low helicopters—this would be an easy mission compared to what they had trained for in the past.

The plan was unconventional, but after hearing it, the planner told O'Boyle to follow him upstairs. Passing through a guarded door and into a secret conference room, O'Boyle entered a meeting that was underway with the Air Force general in charge of planning the air war. The planner told O'Boyle to repeat what he had just told him. Afterward, the idea quickly gained traction and was soon incorporated into the overall war plan.

However, in September—after the president had been briefed on the plan—a large requisition by the special forces team, including twenty-five GPS-equipped ground vehicles, arrived on Schwarzkopf's desk, which sent the general into a fury. Special Operations Command had sensed the leverage they had over the mission and had taken the opportunity to ask for, as one of the planners recalled, "enough equipment to outfit a *third world* country." In addition, Schwarzkopf, who had been a highly decorated conventional soldier in Vietnam, had clashed with special operations forces during the war. In his mind, the "hotshot" units often overstated their capabilities and lacked discipline. He wasn't going to let them jeopardize the success of the war. He deemed the operation too risky and rejected the entire first phase of the air war, telling the planners to come up with a better solution for destroying the radar sites.

In the days that followed, the planners worked continuously to find alternative solutions. To maximize the survival of the follow-on air wave, the attack had to take place in the middle of the night and without moonlight. In the featureless desert, where the winds continually shifted the sand dunes, this made navigation extremely difficult. Captain O'Boyle had another solution—although the GPS satellite constellation was still several years away from full capability, his Pave Low helicopters had been outfitted with GPS receivers that gave them coverage for twenty hours a day. As the only helicopters in the world with both GPS receivers and terrain-following radar, that meant that, provided the timing was right, they would be able to navigate across the featureless desert. Once there, the helicopters could disable the sites using their .50-caliber machine guns equipped with specialized ammunition. The idea was briefed up the chain of command and eventually approved for further development.

The problem with Captain O'Boyle's plan was the lack of firepower—the Pave Low's machine guns didn't have the ability to fully destroy the radar sites, consisting of dozens of vehicles and buildings. An idea was eventually brought up that the Pave Lows could team up with Army AH-64 Apaches: dedicated gunships equipped with Hellfire missiles, Hydra rockets, and much larger 30 mm machine guns—ample firepower to ensure full destruction of the sites. The plan was further refined, and when Schwarzkopf was eventually briefed, it was stressed that without the mixed force, the mission wouldn't be possible.

Despite his dislike for anything labeled "special operations," Schwarzkopf agreed and approved the plan.

The joint team began planning together in the Saudi desert seven hundred miles away from where the attack would be launched. The Pave Lows were led by Lieutenant Colonel Richard Comer of the Twentieth Special Operations Squadron, while the Apaches were led by Lieutenant Colonel Dick Cody of the 101st Airborne Division. Recalling the way the Army and Army Air Corps had successfully worked together during the D-day invasion in World War II, they decided to call their composite organization Task Force Normandy. The force would be broken up into three teams—Red, White, and Blue—who would each be responsible for destroying one of the three early-warning radar sites. Secrecy was paramount, with only those who had a need to know briefed into the mission. As Comer recalls, "I put our best pilot on the job of planning the mission. He and I were the only guys in the squadron to know."

By October, the teams were continuing to train together, logging hundreds of miles each night in preparation for the actual mission.

"All our training was done in a sandbox," said Cody. "We never practiced the route because of the sensitivity of the mission. . . . All their intelligence-gathering networks were up— and everything else. So, this was all done under the umbrella of joint training."

In addition to the tactics, there were significant mechanical challenges to overcome. Helicopters are notoriously high maintenance under even the best conditions. The high temperatures mixed with the blowing sand was wreaking havoc on the sensitive electronics and rotor blades of the helicopters. This required around-the-clock maintenance, including having the ground crews regularly repaint the rotor blades to counter the effects of the abrasive sand. In addition to the mechanical issues, the limited range of the Apaches also posed a problem.

Without a way to top off the tanks, the Apaches wouldn't have enough fuel to strike the targets and return home. Initially, the plan called for a fuel depot to be set up along the border, or potentially even inside Iraq, where the Apaches could land and refuel. This, however, increased the complexity and risked alerting the Iraqis. It also brought back memories of the Desert One catastrophe, where a helicopter crew became engulfed in a dust cloud while refueling and crashed into an aircraft, resulting in the death of eight service members.

One of the youngest pilots on the mission came up with a solution: They could attach a 1,700-pound external fuel tank to the Apache's inboard weapons storage area. The unconventional idea would cost each helicopter a rack of missiles, but it would increase their range enough to prevent them from needing a refueling depot. It was an untested procedure and increased the gross weight of the helicopter to 1,500 pounds past its combat weight; however, the risk was deemed worth it. As a backup, the Pave Low crews were able to come up with a way of transferring fuel from their own helicopters to the Apaches by using fire hoses they had borrowed from local Saudi fire stations. "It was far from a certifiable safe operation, but if we had to use it, we had the helicopters con-figured," said Comer.

By the end of November, with Saddam increasing his threats toward Saudi Arabia as well as the rest of the region, the UN Security Council adopted Resolution 678, setting a January 15 deadline for Iraq's withdrawal from Kuwait through "all necessary means." It was, in effect, an authori-zation for war. By then, the coalition had grown to thirty-nine nations, the largest since World War II, and consisted of nearly a million troops, seven hundred thousand of which were committed by the United States.

The task force continued to train in northern Saudi Arabia. Flying at night without the aid of moonlight was difficult—the helicopters needed to maintain just a three-rotor separa-tion between them while also flying a nap-of-the-earth flight path just fifty feet above the rolling sand dunes. Anything over one hundred feet would allow the radar sites to detect them, putting them at risk of being shot at and compromising the entire opening strike wave. Timing was critical. "It would do no good to hit one radar site and, two minutes later, to hit another one," said Cody. "We had to do it in such a way that we took down critical elements of those radar sites simulta-neously so that Baghdad was not alerted to get their MiG-29s and ground-control intercept systems up."

By December, intelligence had indicated that the third early-warning radar site wasn't connected to the Iraqi air defense system, meaning it didn't need to be destroyed. This allowed the task force to consolidate into just two teams—Red and White. Night after night, they practiced infiltrating denied airspace and attacking two targets simultaneously—often junkyard buses that they turned into smoldering metal. After each run, they would report the level of destruction as Charlie for minimal damage, Bravo for partial destruction, and Alpha for total destruction.

On January 14, Task Force Normandy was ordered to forward deploy to Al Jouf and be in position no later than dark. There still wasn't any information on when the war would start, but with the UN deadline fast approaching, they knew that it would be soon. One of the key indicators of a war starting is large troop movements, which made the task force's flight a challenge. "We even had to do that stealthily, without creating a signature," said Cody. "We rolled into King Khalid Military City—no radio calls or anything—refueled there and took right off. There were already a large number of other helicopters operating out of KKMC, so we would have looked just like any training exercise." Heading out west over the flat terrain, the helicopters dropped low to stay below the radars they would soon be destroying.

THE MISSION

On January 17, 1991, at precisely 12:56 in the morning, four Air Force MH-53 Pave Lows and nine Army AH-64 Apache helicopters took off in two formations as part of Task Force Normandy. With countless hours of training and simulations behind them, the last step was to carry out the mission. "We knew we were poised on the point of history of starting a pretty significant war for our country," said now Major General (retired) Comer. "We had nothing left to do but go fly the mission."

How much resistance they would encounter was still an unknown. "For every 50 Iraqi soldiers, there was expected to be an SA-7 or SA-14 [low-altitude surface-to-air missiles]," said Comer, who flew in one of the Pave Lows. "We anticipated some real danger and possible losses of our MH-53s." On board the Pave Lows were elite Air Force pararescue jumpers in case any of the helicopters went down in the target area. Additional Seahawk and Pave Hawk helicopters were launched to provide support in the event that multiple helicopters went down.

Just after two in the morning, the formations crossed the border into Iraq. "We were tensed and on the lookout as we flew the 40 minutes into Iraq before the war was to start." The helicopters flew just fifty feet above the ground to avoid being detected from the very sites they were set to destroy. Traveling 140 miles per hour without navigation lights in the moonless night and in total radio silence, they traversed the terrain on the way to their targets. "We were seeing stuff for the first time," said Cody. "Most of our training was done on the East Coast of Saudi Arabia where it's very, very flat and you have sand dunes. This was some 700 miles northwest, and it was entirely different. You had mesas and a little bit more terrain, which made it more dangerous."

Shortly after crossing into Iraq, the aviators of White Team watched as the ground in front of them lit up with tracer fire. It was small-arms fire—likely surprised Iraqi soldiers who were blindly shooting at the noise as the helicopters traveled overhead. The helicopters avoided it, but the question was, had the mission been compromised?

After nearly an hour and a half of varying their flight path to avoid any suspected enemy observation positions, the Pave Lows finally arrived at their predesignated drop-off points ten miles away from the radar sites. Dropping infrared chemical lights out the back of the helicopters—visible to only those with night vision goggles—the Pave Lows then veered off to wait for the Apaches.

The Apaches each flew slowly over the lights, updating their navigation systems as they made their way toward the radar sites. They then pulled into their firing positions and hovered five miles away from their targets while the gunners confirmed that the equipment matched the intelligence pictures. Using laser range finders, each Apache developed a firing solution on a different part of the radar site. Finally, the lead Apache pilot broke the silence for the night by keying his radio and broadcasting, "Party in ten." Ten seconds later, all the crews began launching their Hellfire missiles.

After a fifteen-second time of flight, the missiles began detonating against their targets, destroying the generators, command bunkers, and radar dishes. After shooting over forty Hellfire missiles, the Apaches closed into two miles and began shooting Hydra rockets—each containing over a thousand hardened steel fléchettes all taking independent trajectories. In total, they shot over a hundred of the rockets. Finally, they closed in to eight hundred meters and opened up with their chain guns, sending four thousand rounds of high-explosive 30 mm cannon fire against any targets still standing.

"Just incessant fire," said Cody. "Missile after missile, rocket after rocket, 30 mm after 30 mm coming from four aircraft. We engaged their ZPUs [Soviet antiaircraft machine guns] and antiaircraft artillery and put them out. We took those things down in three and a half to four and a half minutes."

The Apaches then closed in over the targets to film the damage. What hadn't exploded in a giant fireball from the fuel reserves detonating had been reduced to smoking ruins. It was total destruction of both sites. The Apaches radioed the outcome to the waiting Pave Lows:

"California—Alpha, Alpha, Alpha."
"Nevada—Alpha, Alpha, Alpha."

The Pave Lows in turn relayed the information via satcom to headquarters where Schwarzkopf responded with, "Thank God."

As the helicopters made their way to the rendezvous point, one of the Pave Lows was shot at by several handheld heat-seeking missiles:

"The SA-7s seemed to be fired accurately," said Comer. "The crew members of the Pave Low called out the inbound missiles. [They] made the call for the helicopters to break and to jettison some flares to decoy the missiles. . . . The jinking of the helicopters, plus the IRCMs [infrared countermeasures], seemed to be what made the missiles miss the helicopters."

As the two formations of helicopters made their way back, they could see the hundreds of aircraft that made up the first strike wave streaming across the border.

"You could look off to the south and there were blinkers lined up," said the pilot of the lead Pave Low. "You could see a long way on goggles. And it's also desert, so it's clear. There were anti-collision lights lined up; it looked like an LA freeway. . . . And they were all chasing these big blinkers . . . the tankers. Then all of a sudden, there was a point where there were no more lights. So, they would get gas, drop off, turn lights off, and head north."

One of the fighter pilots in the strike wave later wrote a letter to the crews of Task Force Normandy and said, "During our [mission] brief, we noticed our route of flight took us right over an active radar site. . . . We were told not to worry about it. We saw the explosions and your helicopters in our FLIR as we flew over you. There was immense relief!"

"The Iraqis now had no eyes to see with over a large portion of their border," said Comer. "I do not believe anybody detected our initial wave of fighters going into Iraq."

Shortly after the early-warning radar sites were destroyed, waves of fighter aircraft from the Air Force and Navy destroyed key air defense centers throughout the country. To prevent a coordinated national defense, they struck military command bunkers, the presidential grounds, and Iraq's main telephone exchange along with other key communications nodes. Simultaneously, fifty-two Tomahawk missiles struck other critical targets throughout the country: A third of them struck the national electrical grid, shutting down power to the country's air defense systems, while the rest went after other core targets, such as missile support facilities and Saddam himself.

After the helicopters crossed back into Saudi Arabia, the task force dissolved—the Apaches flew back to base while the Pave Lows immediately transitioned to their search-and-rescue mission. Computer modeling analysis being done at the Pentagon projected more than 125 pilots would need to be rescued after being shot down.

"We were very surprised that there were no shoot-downs reported to us the first night," said Comer. "We learned later that one Navy plane went down under fire with the wingman reporting it exploded and no expectation of a survivor. My expectation was 2 percent losses among the fighters. These were realistic expectations that I think all the generals had signed up to."

For the next forty-two consecutive days and nights, coalition airpower subjected Iraq to one of the most intensive air bombardments in military history. Launching nearly one hundred thousand sorties, primarily from Saudi Arabia along with six carrier battlegroups stationed in the Persian Gulf, the coalition quickly decimated KARI along with the rest of the Iraqis' air defense system, depriving Saddam of the ability to control his forces. In the past, such as during the Iran-Iraq War, Saddam had micromanaged his forces, often discouraging initiative at lower levels. Now, without guidance, his forces quickly crumbled.

After decimating the Iraqi military from the air, the ground war began on February 26. Thousands of tanks and infantry fighting vehicles streamed across the border, piercing the Iraqi defenses. Three of the largest tank battles in American history ensued, with equally lopsided victories for the coalition. They quickly expelled Iraqi forces out of Kuwait while U.S., British, and French forces continued to pursue them across the border into Iraq, leaving a trail of destruction that became known as the Highway of Death. On February 28, one hundred hours after the ground campaign started, President Bush declared a cease-fire, ending combat operations and bringing a close to the war.

Ultimately, the Gulf War would go down as one of the most decisive one-sided victories in modern history. Although the coalition had significant numerical and technological advantages, the results were still shocking. During the war, nearly 200,000 Iraqi soldiers were either killed or captured. The coalition, however, only lost 292 soldiers, of which half were lost during pre- or postwar accidents, an unprecedented ratio that had never even been approached in the history of armed conflict.

While there are several factors that contributed to the coalition's overwhelming victory, one of the primary reasons was a new system of thinking that encouraged creative decision-making called *effects-based operations*. Instead of the traditional means of conducting wars, which relied on each side sending their forces to fight each other, often in bloody wars of attrition, effects-based operations was a process for obtaining desired outcomes through a synergistic approach toward defeating the enemy. By treating the enemy as a system and identifying the relationships within that system, the coalition could then target weaknesses that would have an outsize influence on the enemy.

Throughout history, military commanders have always

sought conditions that would achieve their objectives. However, by the Gulf War, the rapid advancement of technology had finally enabled effects-based operations to be used throughout an entire war plan. New developments in communication, intelligence gathering, and theory enabled a better understanding of the complex relationships at play within an enemy country. This understanding was then used to identify vulnerable strategic targets, which, with the advent of stealth aircraft and smart weapons, could then be precisely destroyed. This enabled planners to attack many targets simultaneously, leading to *parallel warfare*, known in the media as "shock and awe"—an overwhelming display of force that paralyzes the enemy's ability to operate.

The core of effects-based operations was the clear separation between the enemy's forces and the objectives. In combat, it's easy to get lured into the trap of forces competing against each other—aircraft versus aircraft, tanks versus tanks, soldiers versus soldiers; however, effects-based operations didn't care what was producing the effect, only that it was achieved. If an important communication node needed to be taken down, it could be destroyed by a bomb, which would have been the traditional solution, or it could be jammed, cyberattacked, sabotaged, raided, or any one of many solutions. If other sources of power, such as diplomatic, informational, or economic leverage could be applied more effectively, then the military didn't even need to be used.

For the Gulf War, effects-based operations were tightly integrated throughout its planning and execution. As Colonel John Warden, one of the leading airpower theorists whose concept became the heart of the Desert Storm campaign, said:

> As a planner or commander, you ought to be able to tell what each bomb has got to do with the peace that you want to follow the war. If you can't tell how a given bomb relates to the peace that's going to follow, then you probably haven't done your homework well and you probably shouldn't drop that particular bomb.

During the war, military leaders were freer than ever before to combine the best elements from land, sea, space, and cyber to find solutions. This had the effect of unleashing their creative potential, resulting in the decimation of the Iraqi military.

Today, effects-based operations is the standard for planning and executing missions. It's a guiding framework that enables more effective and efficient solutions. It facilitates problem-solving across disciplines, organizations, and levels. It's one of the key factors that's helped the military overcome the notorious infighting between services. The concept is not just relevant for the military but is a mindset and guide, like agile project management that can be applied throughout all levels of an organization to unlock creative potential. Here are the overarching principles:

1. Tasks and operations should be driven by the desired end states

An effects-based approach should start with the desired outcomes and work backward. This enables an integrated strategy throughout the planning and execution that supports the objectives. Often, large gains in effectiveness and efficiency can be realized by synchronizing operations. When looked at from the big picture, many processes are often redundant and can therefore be eliminated. This mentality runs counter to the way many organizations operate, where planning starts with a given set of resources and capabilities and then transitions to what can be accomplished with them.

Working backward, always with the desired outcome in mind, can help prevent the planning and execution from devolving into becoming excessively process-driven. When this happens, people become narrowly focused and lose sight of the big picture, reducing their flexibility and creativity. The larger the organization, the more people will be naturally drawn toward focusing on their narrow problem set, requiring a greater weight of effort by leadership on *why* the effects are being generated.

Task Force Normandy adhered to this tenet closely by identifying the KARI air defense system as the primary means for the Iraqis to detect a coalition attack. Once identified, intelligence analysts found the weakest link in the system—two remote radar outposts in the middle of the desert. Only then did they begin to devise a way to disable them.

The lesson can be found in business as well—fulfilling a customer's need should be the desired end state. Despite how revolutionary a new technology may be, without a clear need for it, it's difficult for it to become a commercial success. This need may be forecasted or may not even be consciously known by the customer; however, every product must eventually pass the test of satisfying a customer's need.

Starting at the end goal and working backward is also the path to individual mastery. Hard work and talent aren't enough to become a top performer in a field. A clear and efficient plan for how to get there is necessary. By identifying the end state for a new skill you're learning, you can then develop a plan that integrates into your current skill set and maximizes your potential.

2. Effects over tools

An effects-based approach focuses on the cause and effect of each action taken so that the end state can ultimately be achieved. The goal is to break down the requirement to the point where it's not tied to a specific tool or process. The mistake that many people and organizations make is having a preconceived notion of what resources they need to use to solve a given problem. However, the tool or process used is not nearly as important as the effects it generates.

Task Force Normandy is a great example of this—traditional doctrine would have never used helicopters to carry out the initial strikes of a major war. However, the planners, instead of focusing on the tools available, focused on the effects they needed. They established that they needed to (1) find the radar sites in the remote desert at night, (2) remain undetected, (3) destroy the sites, and (4) receive confirmation that the sites had been destroyed. Once these effects were established, the most efficient means that emerged was something that had never been done before: pairing Air Force Pave Lows with Army Apaches to form a task force.

The lesson of effects over tools and processes is relevant to businesses as well. A product represents hundreds of concepts that need to be packaged together with varying trade-offs. Tightly fitting all the concepts together to create a great product is the challenge. From the beginning, there will be large, immovable constraints that need to be worked around. These constraints are often physics-based—there's only so much you can do with materials and electronics. Other constraints will be easier to navigate; however, they'll still come with varying levels of difficulty. By breaking requirements down into small, desired effects, we can then recombine them into a more efficient and effective way of solving a customer's needs.

The same is true for everyday decisions. If you need a way to travel to work, the requirement shouldn't simply be a car. Instead, it should be broken down into effects needed, such as commute time, cost, number of passengers, reliability, ease of use, and so on. Once we've broken down the problem into the effects needed, we can potentially find an innovative solution that's more effective, such as a car service, rideshare, public transportation, truck, or any one of many solutions. While a car may ultimately be the best option, breaking down the requirement into effects needed gives us at least an opportunity to explore alternative solutions.

3. Find solutions that encompass the effects

Decision-making is about finding the best solution among alternatives. If there's only one solution, then there isn't a decision to make. The question is: How do we generate alternatives from which we can then assess the expected value? This ability is called *creativity* and is often treated as an innate talent. While there is some truth to that, there's a framework that can significantly aid in finding innovative solutions.

So far, we've talked about the first step—breaking down requirements into effects. If a specific tool or process is tied to a requirement, then it doesn't lend itself to finding alternative solutions. However, once we've broken down the problem into the required effects, then we can find solutions that encompass as many of them as possible. This stage is a difficult process for most people—there's a tendency to quickly be drawn away from the ill-defined to the well-defined.

Finding alternatives is an ill-defined and messy process, which gives people the illusion that they're not making progress toward their end goal. This can be further exacerbated by attempting to measure the progress. This leads to an overly quick selection of an obvious solution that's worked in the past, which may not be the most effective solution for the current situation. In a group setting without a structured approach, once these obvious solutions are identified, they serve to anchor the remaining discussion and prevent a thorough development of alternatives. While it's possible that a solution may instantly come to mind that satisfies all needed effects, more often it's a slow, structured process that will eventually bring it into focus.

The first step to generating alternatives is to prioritize the required effects in numerical order. Once this is accomplished, solutions can be identified that satisfy only the most important effect—don't worry about the rest. Many of these alternatives will, of course, be terrible when measured against all the required effects; however, this process helps to remove our strong bias toward immediately optimizing. This step is particularly effective in group settings where people are often afraid to fail. Developing solutions that meet all needed effects can be incredibly difficult; however, finding solutions for just one effect is substantially easier. This enables easy wins for people, leading to more engagement and more alternatives. Once solutions have been identified for the most important effect, the process should be repeated for subsequent effects.

The next step is to identify alternatives that satisfy just the top two needed effects. The overlapping requirements will dramatically pare down the number of viable solutions. This process should be repeated until you're only left with alternatives that satisfy all the needed effects. Keep in mind that it's impossible to generate every conceivable alternative, so until you reach the good idea cutoff line, continue to keep an open mind for new solutions. Often there's an opportunity to create a hybrid alternative that recombines the best elements of what you've already come up with. Once this is done, you can then judge all your alternatives based on their effectiveness and efficiency of achieving your objective.

4. Uncertainty means you must be flexible

One of the tenets of effects-based operations is that the world is comprised of complex and adaptive systems colliding with each other to create a dynamic and often unpredictable environment. Small changes in the inputs can create unexpectedly large outputs. While an effects-based approach should focus on how all actions are driving an end state, it's a mistake to think we can predict the future with any certainty.

The interactions of relationships are often nonlinear and on the edge of tipping points. New and unanticipated behaviors are likely to emerge as systems interact. An effects-based approach, therefore, should anticipate change and, above all, remain flexible.

In the aftermath of the success of Desert Storm, many believed that we were on the cusp of being able to predict the precise outcome of wars before the first shot was fired. With the exponential increase in computing power, they believed that models could be built to accurately forecast the interaction of the world around us. However, there's a large difference between following an effects-based approach to planning and attempting to precisely forecast the future.

One of the most difficult variables is understanding how people will react. The human mind represents perhaps the greatest source of uncertainty for anyone attempting to build a predictive model. Humans are adept at finding new and innovative solutions that have never been conceived. They then leverage technology, resources, and manpower to create an outsize advantage, purposely creating as many butterfly effects as possible. Take a showdown that occurred several years after the Gulf War between the United States' premier attack aircraft, the F-117 stealth fighter, and an obsolete 1950s-era surface-to-air missile site.

THE NIGHTHAWK

On March 27, 1999, an aircraft, piloted by Colonel Dale Zelko, took off into a cloud-filled, full-moon night. This was the fourth day of Operation Allied Force—the air war over the former Republic of Yugoslavia. Colonel Zelko, a decorated veteran of Desert Storm, was at the controls of one of the most innovative aircraft ever developed: the F-117 Nighthawk.

The Nighthawk was unlike any previous aircraft design. Built around the principle that stealth was the single most important attribute, it was the culmination of twenty years of progress, dating back to a Soviet mathematician's paper on why an airplane's radar return was related more to its shape than its size.

As radar technology advanced, it became increasingly difficult to penetrate deep into an enemy's airspace. An aircraft could no longer hope to fly low enough to avoid detection. Similarly, surface-to-air missile technology had developed to the point where high-altitude aircraft were now obsolete. What was needed was a way to defeat the radar itself.

In 1975, engineers from the famed Skunk Works laboratory—designers of the SR-71 Blackbird and the U-2 Dragon Lady—began designing an aircraft that would be nearly invisible to radar. From the beginning, it was a top-secret black project, meaning it was unacknowledged by the government. To achieve the stealth design, they used supercomputer modeling to arrange the surfaces of the aircraft in such a way that radar energy, upon hitting the aircraft, would scatter at odd angles, preventing most of it from returning back to the radar.

Further reducing the aircraft's radar signature, an exotic coating containing tiny spheres of carbonyl iron was applied to the skin. As radar energy hit the aircraft, the coating converted the energy into heat, which then dissipated into the airstream. To mask its heat signature, tiles from the space shuttle were used throughout the bottom of the aircraft.

To test the design, they secretly transported a mock-up into the Mojave Desert and placed it on a large stand. Although it was less than a mile away from the radar—extremely short range by aircraft standards—nothing appeared on the radar screen when they turned it on. The engineers, believing that their radar was broken, began troubleshooting it when a bird happened to land on the mock-up, visually registering on their radar screen. The radar was, in fact, working—the engineers had succeeded in designing an aircraft so stealthy that it couldn't even be seen by their own testing equipment.

The F-117 remained an unacknowledged program for nearly a decade, with almost no one, even inside the government, knowing of its existence. It was America's silver bullet against the Soviet Union during the Cold War. Its primary mission was to penetrate deep into enemy air defenses and drop nuclear weapons on the most highly protected and valuable targets.

The aircraft was considered such an advantage for the United States that extreme lengths were taken to ensure its existence was hidden. Its pilots were assigned to the aging A-7 Corsair II at the remote Tonopah Test Range in the Nevada desert. During the day, they flew sorties in the A-7, under the guise that they were testing new avionics systems. Once the sun set, though—under the cover of darkness and away from watchful Soviet spies and satellites—they transitioned to flying the diamond-shaped F-117. The program was so secret that when one crashed in 1986, igniting a small forest fire, the Air Force established a restricted airspace while armed guards blocked entry into the area, to include the firefighters. Helicopter gunships circled the site while the debris was collected and then replaced with the remains of a different type of aircraft.

The F-117's baptism by fire came during Desert Storm in 1991. There, it dominated the Iraqi military. Despite making up less than 3 percent of the coalition aircraft, F-117s destroyed over 30 percent of the targets on the first night. They primarily struck targets in Baghdad, where—despite over sixteen thousand surface-to-air missiles, seven thousand antiaircraft guns, and eight hundred fighter aircraft defending the city—*zero* F-117s were lost throughout the war.

THE ENEMY

On the opposing side of the battlefield, a Serbian named Zoltán Dani was in charge of an aging SA-3 surface-to-air missile battalion. The SA-3 was a Soviet ground-based missile system designed in the late 1950s to shoot down enemy aircraft. When it debuted, it disappointingly had a shorter range, a lower engagement altitude, and slower missiles than its predecessors. Its fragile and complicated design prevented it from being mobile, making it extremely vulnerable to attack. By the mid-1990s, the SA-3 had become obsolete and relegated to second-tier militaries like the Yugoslavian army.

Dani did, however, have experience. Twenty years prior, during the 1982 Lebanon War, he had seen Israeli fighters destroy twenty-nine out of thirty surface-to-air missile sites in less than two hours. This led him to develop new tactics to increase the survivability of his battalion. He started by breaking the system down into pieces small enough to fit on trucks. Though the SA-3 wasn't intended to be mobile, he found that with extensive training, his troops could pack up the site in ninety minutes. This allowed him to move several times a day, making it difficult for Allied forces to find him.

He also understood that the primary threat to him was HARM missiles launched by NATO escort aircraft. These missiles homed in on radar but became unguided as soon as the radar was turned off. Therefore, he made it a strict rule that his radar would only turn on twice for twenty seconds at a time. If his battalion couldn't shoot down an aircraft, they would prioritize survival and start the process of relocating.

Dani found that his SA-3 radar had a similar electronic signature to the radar in a MiG-21 aircraft. Yugoslavia happened to have several MiG-21s in storage after they seized them from Iraq during the Gulf War. Dani had his men strip the radars from the abandoned aircraft and placed them on the outskirts of his battalion, away from anything of value. Whenever his radar was operating, he would turn on the repurposed MiG radars to decoy any incoming missiles away from his valuable equipment and operators.

Dani also embedded spies around NATO air bases in the region so that when aircraft took off before a mission, they could relay the information, effectively giving him warning of impending strikes. And because only a small percentage of aircraft could carry the deadly HARM missiles, he could further assess his risk based on the type of aircraft that took off.

THE MISSION

Colonel Zelko lifted off into the night sky in his F-117 and quickly entered the clouds. The weather was poor, causing many of the other NATO aircraft to be grounded. This was the fourth night of the war, with the stealth planes having already taken out many key parts of the Yugoslavian air defense. Colonel Zelko was a veteran of the F-117; nearly a decade earlier during Desert Storm, he had destroyed hardened targets while being shot at by dozens of surface-to-air missiles and hundreds of antiaircraft-artillery sites—none of which came close to hitting him.

After topping off with fuel from an airborne tanker, Colonel Zelko and several other F-117s pushed toward Croatia. Before they flew over the coastline, they "stealth upped"—a term the pilots used to describe retracting all exterior antennas and cutting transmissions from their aircraft, making them nearly invisible to the enemy. They then split up, all on separate courses toward their targets deep within the country.

On the ground, Dani had received word that a strike wave had taken off. Because of the bureaucracy of NATO mission planning, the flight routes were nearly identical for each mission. After three days of watching similar strike waves, Dani knew where to point his radar and when to turn it on.

As Colonel Zelko made his way into Kosovo toward his targets in downtown Belgrade, Dani began seeing faint hints of the aircraft on his early-warning radar. The vintage radar set—which used vacuum tubes instead of modern transistors—picked up what looked like a ghost on the screen. Though he couldn't shoot the aircraft with this radar, it allowed him to further refine the route and timing for his primary targeting radar. Once the aircraft was fifteen miles away, Dani ordered his targeting radar to turn on. For twenty seconds, the operators tried to find the invisible aircraft; however, they failed to find it. Dani, sensing the opportunity slipping away, immediately ordered the radar back on. Again, the operators tried desperately to find the aircraft, as the seconds ticked down. Once the timer hit zero, they shut down the radar, knowing they had failed and now had to start the process of relocating.

Up to this point in the conflict, Dani had never operated his radar for more than forty seconds without moving to a different site, assuming that the escort aircraft would take about a minute to find and shoot him. However, this night was different: Dani knew, through his network of spies, that many of the escort aircraft, tasked with protecting the F-117s, likely hadn't taken off due to the poor weather. Therefore, he broke his own rule and ordered the radar back on for a third time.

At 8:15 p.m. local time, with a range of just eight miles, Dani finally found Colonel Zelko's F-117 just as he opened his weapons-bay doors to release his bombs. The large increase in radar signature allowed him to develop a stable track on the aircraft. With the radar now tracking its target and well within range of the missiles, Dani ordered two launches in quick succession.

Meanwhile, Colonel Zelko, having hit his targets, began turning back toward the coastline. A little over a minute later, he spotted the missiles. In an after-action report, he stated:

> The missiles were moving at three times the speed of sound, so there wasn't much time to react. Just before the first missile reached me, I closed my eyes and turned my head, anticipating the impact. I knew there would be a fireball, and I didn't want to be blinded. I felt the first one go right over me, so close that it rocked the aircraft. Then I opened my eyes and turned my head, and there was the other missile. The impact was violent. A huge flash of light and heat engulfed my plane and blew off the left wing, sending the plane into a roll. If you're in an airplane that hits some turbulence and you feel a little light in your feet, you're momentarily at zero g's. I was at negative seven g's. My body was being pulled out of the seat upward toward the canopy. As I strained to reach the ejection handles, one thought crossed my mind: This is really, really, really bad.

The explosion of the missile was so large that it was seen by an airborne tanker flying over Bosnia nearly one hundred miles away. This actually contributed to Colonel Zelko's survival—once he ejected from the tumbling aircraft, he was able to quickly contact the tanker, whose crew had already begun search-and-rescue procedures upon seeing the fireball. Minutes later, he landed in a field south of the town of Ruma, about a mile from where his aircraft crashed. For the next eight hours, Colonel Zelko hid in a drainage ditch, where, during a search of the area, enemy soldiers at one point came within several hundred meters of him. Likely minutes away from being captured, he was rescued via helicopter by a U.S. combat search-and-rescue team.

CREATIVITY CAN BE AN EXPONENTIAL ADVANTAGE

Zoltán Dani's missile battalion was able to shoot down one of the most technologically advanced aircraft because of his creativity and ingenuity. He found nontraditional solutions to overcome a forty-year technological gap. He systematically prioritized and solved problems to enable his battalion to survive throughout the war while continuing to disrupt NATO war plans. During the seventy-eight-day war, his supposedly unmovable missile site traveled over fifty thousand miles throughout the Yugoslavian countryside, continually frustrating NATO planners. His mobility, minimal radar use, and homemade decoys presented a major problem for NATO forces, who, despite launching nearly a hundred HARM missiles at him, never succeeded in neutralizing his battalion. This prevented the freedom of movement that NATO planners had expected, keeping most of their aircraft far away from the battlefield and ineffective. Just over a month after Dani shot down the F-117, his missile battalion would go on to prove that it wasn't a fluke by shooting down another aircraft, this time a U.S. F-16 flown by a decorated fighter pilot who would later go on to become the Chief of Staff of the Air Force.

NATO war planners were just as responsible as Dani for losing the F-117. The tight control by NATO leadership regarding flight routes led to attacks always emanating from the same direction. Poor operational security also enabled enemy spotters to see aircraft taking off, which often gave hours of lead time for the enemy. After several days of similar operations, enemy missile operators could deduce the approximate time, location, altitude, and direction of attacks, which made it significantly easier to close the technological gap with NATO's advanced airpower. These problems were quickly identified by the pilots flying the missions; however, NATO orders were built too inflexibly to allow innovation and refinement by the aircrews.

In the aftermath of the Kosovo air campaign, effects-based operations were updated to account for uncertainty by dramatically increasing the flexibility of the war fighters. By the time I began flying missions over Afghanistan, pilots had far more influence on the decision-making process. Our orders, known as *air tasking orders,* were treated as a rough guide that could be modified as conditions required. Technology had enabled a quicker dissemination of information by senior leaders so that war fighters could make decisions that were in line with their overall intent. This enabled me, while I was flying, to speak directly with higher headquarters, allowing my high-fidelity tactical view to be combined with their strategic view, to produce the best actions to drive specific effects.

On nearly every flight, I altered my orders, and on at least a dozen occasions, I completely changed missions based on the information I had in my cockpit. While ultimately headquarters was in charge, this tenet of flexibility meant that I could quickly innovate and fill in any gaps in the planning that they had missed.

Creativity is one of the few resources that can provide an exponential advantage to those who are able to harness it. This advantage is currently playing out during the ongoing war between Russia and Ukraine. Despite Russian aggression against Georgia, Syria, and the annexation of the Crimea, until recently there had been little backlash from NATO and other world powers against the country. This, however, changed when Russia invaded Ukraine.

Led by Volodymyr Zelenskyy, Ukraine was able to innovate and systematically harness modern forms of communication to rally support from countries around the world. They immediately seized the narrative by leveraging social media to showcase the atrocities committed by Russia while also uniting their population's will to fight behind myths such as the Ghost of Kyiv, a fighter pilot who shot down six Russian aircraft during the opening days of the war, and the legend of Snake Island, a unit that was destroyed after telling the Russians to "go f**k yourself." Although many of the stories have been proven to be significantly embellished, the effects were still achieved—they overcame Russia's extensive propaganda, gained the moral high ground, and proved to their population and the world that they had a chance at repelling the former superpower. This created a landslide of support from the international community, who have since gone on to place stifling sanctions on Russia while providing critical resources for Ukraine to keep fighting.

The spirt of creativity and innovation has played on the battlefield as well. Ukrainian teenagers innovated by turning their drones into Molotov cocktail bombers. Farmers used their tractors to drag Russian tanks away from their operators. The Ukrainian military decimated Russian armor and low-flying aircraft using swift ambushes, armed with handheld rocket launchers. The Russians, however, were paralyzed by their inflexibility. They struggled with maneuver warfare, supply logistics, vehicles breaking down, and secure communications—the very basics of any military operation. This allowed Ukraine—a country with roughly ten times fewer soldiers, equipment, and funding—to repel the Russians from most of their country.

We often treat creativity as an innate talent; however, it can be developed and enhanced. Creativity is simply connecting things in nontraditional ways. While some people are naturally good at innovating solutions, most people and all organizations would benefit from a process and framework for how to break down problems in a way that lends itself to creative solutions.

Effects-based operations is one of the best tools for enabling creative decision-making. However, when using it, people need to understand that the world is full of uncertainty, and precisely predicting the future is an impossible task. The antidote, therefore, is embracing uncertainty and building flexibility into any plans.

When making decisions, we're just trying to skew the

odds in our favor—some good decisions won't work out, while other bad ones will. This element of luck is unavoidable; however, over time, those who have a systematic approach for finding and evaluating solutions will give themselves a significant advantage, whether it's on the battlefield, in the boardroom, or in their personal lives.

MENTAL TOUGHNESS

Parwan Province, Afghanistan: 1530 Local Time

As I sat in the intelligence brief, an Army officer gave me an update on a high-risk operation that several special forces teams were conducting in Nangarhar Province in eastern Afghanistan. ISIS had spread into the country and were beginning to grow roots along the Pakistani border. They were terrorizing the civilian population with brutal killings and forcing teenagers to act as suicide bombers against NATO forces. Within weeks, their growth threatened to destabilize the country. Our orders, straight from the Secretary of Defense, were to "annihilate them."

The plan was simple: Ground forces would start at the northernmost town of ISIS-controlled territory and would conduct a clearing operation, forcing them to retreat south into the desolate mountains, where air support could then be unleashed on them. This multi-week operation was considered high risk—the teams would have to dismount from their vehicles and walk through the towns. To minimize casualties, the towns had already been evacuated, but many of the inhabitants were either unable or unwilling to leave their homes. To protect the civilians, our rules of engagement needed to give the benefit of the doubt to anyone still residing in the area. That meant that our firepower was severely restricted, often giving ISIS fighters an opportunity to shoot at NATO forces first.

Air support would be a key advantage: The plan called for a mix of coverage from Apache helicopters, AC-130 gunships, and F-16s to provide around-the-clock firepower for the teams on the ground. There would also be dozens of surveillance aircraft monitoring the area and scouting ahead of the clearing operation. Because we were the only fighter squadron in the country, in order to provide twenty-four-hour coverage, we could only launch two F-16s every four hours.

The first week of the operation went relatively smoothly: The teams came under daily fire; however, their superior equipment and training allowed them to effectively engage the enemy at range. Flying overhead, we worked with the imbedded Air Force combat controllers—some of the most elite special forces soldiers in the world—to take out the enemy. Using a mix of five-hundred- and two-thousand-pound bombs along with laser rockets, we developed into a lethal team that could quickly clear an area. Over time, we developed relationships with the combat controllers, where, despite never meeting them or knowing their names, we could identify each of them by their voices and knew how they operated.

As my wingman and I sat in the intelligence brief, the

Army officer gave us updates from the previous twenty-four hours since we had last flown. We charted the current position of the teams and went over where they had taken fire from. We then watched the cockpit recordings from the previous day's strikes so that we could glean any lessons learned on how the enemy tactics were evolving and how we could be more effective. Midway through the brief, we were interrupted by the operations supervisor. There was a firefight underway—the ground team had been ambushed while entering a new village. The current aircraft providing overwatch were running low on weapons, and we needed to take off as soon as possible to replace them.

We quickly began gearing up. I put on my G suit, harness, and survival vest. The last step always involved me taking my M9 pistol out of the holster and clipping it into the survival vest holster along with a spare magazine in case I had to eject over the hostile countryside. We then made our way out to our jets. Once we started them, we had our weapons armed and then quickly took off. Flying in full afterburner and just under the speed of sound, we made our way east. As soon as we were within communication range, I checked in with the other two-ship of F-16s who were low on fuel and out of weapons. They passed on to us the location of the friendlies and where they had already engaged the enemy as they peeled off and made their way back home. We then switched over our radios to the combat controller's encrypted frequency so we could begin coordinating with them.

The first thing we heard were the Apaches checking off— they were low on fuel and on their way home. Because of their slow speed—roughly twice that of a car on the highway—we wouldn't see them for the rest of our mission. This was a big loss; Apaches are one of the most valuable close-air-support assets—unlike fighters that orbit tens of thousands of feet up at high speed, the helicopters were right with the troops on the ground. They could easily follow their movements and maneuver with them. Combined with their large weapons loadout, this made them highly effective within the confines of a town or village.

Next, we heard coordination going on between the combat controller on the ground and the other aircraft in the stack. The *stack* is the airspace directly above an operation. Sometimes there are fifteen aircraft all orbiting in support of a single operation. To deconflict and prevent the aircraft from running into each other—or dropping bombs on one another—an aircraft will get a block of altitude, say, from fifteen thousand to seventeen thousand feet, to operate in. In the stack today were several surveillance aircraft and an unmanned Predator drone above us. Below us was the fearsome AC-130 gunship, a converted cargo aircraft with a 25 mm Gatling gun, a 40 mm automatic cannon, and a massive 105 mm howitzer cannon, making it essentially a flying battleship.

I had worked with this controller before, and one of the things I noticed was that even during a firefight, he was always calm. This time, though, his voice was tense. He rapidly called out areas for the AC-130 to scan out ahead of the team. As we checked in with him, he gave us an update on their position and plan as well as the suspected buildings the enemy was hiding in.

The first few minutes of an overwatch mission are always

the most difficult. No matter how thoroughly the plan has been briefed, it's always challenging to rapidly gain situational awareness of where the friendly forces are, where the enemy is, and where everyone is moving next. No plan survives first contact with the enemy, which means there are always changes that need to be overcome while airborne. To add to the complexity, friendly Afghan army forces were now intermixed within the U.S. special forces teams, making it difficult to keep track of everyone involved.

Like a doctor's Hippocratic oath, our first job when flying close air support is to do no harm to friendly forces. A *fratricide,* as we call it, whereby we accidentally kill or wound a friendly soldier, is the worst thing that we can possibly do. It's a fate worse than death: to know that a fellow service member has been maimed or killed because of a mistake you made is unforgivable. Even in training, to simulate shooting the wrong aircraft or dropping a bomb on the wrong target is taken seriously and swiftly punished.

Unfortunately, over the years, there've been many fratricides due to the difficulty of combining airpower in close proximity to friendly forces on the ground. A modern fighter carries an incredible amount of firepower, which means that your decisions are amplified. A rifle fired by a soldier and a bomb dropped by a fighter are both controlled by a single person. The bullet from the rifle may kill one person, whereas the bomb, depending on its size, can kill everyone within several hundred feet.

As my wingman and I split off to opposite sides of our orbit around the target, I heard the radio crackle to life and the controller start yelling, "We're taking fire, extremely accurate fire!" In the background, I could hear automatic weapons being discharged while another soldier was yelling where the gunfire came from.

The controller called on the AC-130 to engage the enemy. The lumbering aircraft, several thousand feet below me and circling in the opposite direction, began opening fire as the discharge gases created a trail of smoke behind it. Looking at the ground, I could see what looked like sparks as the hundreds of rounds impacted the field where the ISIS soldiers were shooting from.

After about fifteen seconds, the controller said, "Viper"— that was my call sign—"we need bombs now, stand by for a nine-line." A *nine-line* is the name we use to coordinate an airstrike. We were the only aircraft loaded out to destroy buildings; the AC-130, despite its firepower, didn't have the penetrating capability to take them out. He then passed me the location of a building they were taking fire from. I pulled up the coordinates, confirmed we were talking about the same building, and rolled in on the target. I flipped up the master arm switch, fired my laser to pass precise ranging to the bomb, and then hit the red weapons-release button, sending a five-hundred-pound bomb hurtling toward the target. Forty-five seconds later, the building exploded as a cloud of smoke replaced where it had just stood.

About this time, the AC-130's radios completely went down. They could no longer communicate with anyone. The combat controller tried several times to call in additional fire from the AC-130, and I could hear desperation in his voice as he said, "We need immediate fire, now!" After several moments of silence, he turned to us and began passing us additional targets.

Over the next five minutes, my wingman and I dropped several more five-hundred-pound bombs. We were stopping the brunt of the ISIS fighters' attack and pushing them back across a dry riverbed. It was then that I heard over the radio that one of the soldiers had been hit. "It's bad. . . . It's not looking good for him," said the controller.

The second-worst fate, behind a fratricide, is losing a soldier that you are providing overwatch for. When you're providing close air support, those soldiers are the reason why you're there. They're relying on you to protect them. Their families are relying on you to protect them. Going through flight training, I would hear my instructors talk about the number of combat missions they had flown and how they had brought back every soldier they had provided overwatch for. As soon as I heard the controller talking about the downed soldier, I felt a knot form in my stomach.

STRESS

We have a saying in the fighter pilot community that you lose twenty IQ points as soon as you put on your helmet. That means that what looks easy in the classroom is much more difficult when you're sweating in the hot cockpit, with dozens of people talking simultaneously through the radios and lives at stake. Emotions significantly affect our decision-making ability. Biologically, we've evolved so that the rational part of our brains, known as the neocortex, is intertwined with our limbic systems, responsible for emotion. This makes it easy for us to believe we're behaving rationally, when, in fact, we've been hijacked by our emotions.

Humans have, on average, over sixty thousand thoughts a day, with upward of 85 percent of those thoughts spent on fear-based planning—that is, worrying about things that might happen in the future. We've likely evolved this way because, in our past, death was all around us. If we broke our leg, there was almost no chance that we would survive. Even social decisions were a matter of life and death. Tribes were under constant warfare. Analyzing stone-aged skeletons, archeologists estimate that 25 percent of all deaths back then occurred due to homicide—a staggering rate that's 20,000 percent higher than today. If you were ostracized from those around you, there was little to no chance of you surviving on your own. This brutal existence led to us having a conservative mentality that is ill-adapted for the modern world.

When our brain's amygdala senses danger, it activates stress and fear hormones, such as adrenaline and cortisol. As our bodies prepare for action, our liver releases glucose to provide additional energy for our muscles. Cortisol increases our blood sugar level while decreasing our immune system functioning. Our digestive system begins to shut down, which is what gives us a butterfly sensation, or knot, in our stomach. Our lungs begin working harder, preparing for an increase in oxygen demand, which causes fast, shallow breaths as well as dry mouth and difficulty swallowing. As the adrenaline enters our bloodstream, it causes our heartbeat to quicken while flushing our chest, neck, and face with a warm sensation.

However, this increase in physical readiness comes at a cost. Our prefrontal cortex—the most advanced part of our brain that's responsible for high-order cognitive abilities—begins to shut down. Working memory decreases, while attention switches from a thoughtful top-down approach based on prioritization to a bottom-up approach, where we easily become fixated on the most stimulating sensation.

The Air Force began studying this transformation after the Second World War based on observations that pilots who were highly skilled during peacetime sorties often crashed their planes in the heat of battle due to simple mental errors. Over the years, the Air Force has conducted several studies focused on how stress affects pilots. The results have shown that while stress exposure can slightly increase performance for simple, well-rehearsed tasks, it *severely* reduces performance for tasks that require complex or flexible thinking.

As an instructor pilot, I see this all the time with student pilots. In fact, it happened while writing this book. I was flying with an above-average student who had come straight from pilot training, meaning he was inexperienced and in his midtwenties. Before the flight, he was able to easily answer all the questions I asked him. During the flight, he did a good job of leading us out to the airspace and dogfighting against me. On the way home, however, things began to unravel. We were instructed by the control tower to change frequencies, a simple task that's done dozens of times throughout a flight. The student, however, inadvertently changed to the wrong frequency. The F-35 is unique because it has a large touch screen display, like two giant iPads fused together, in place of the traditional dials and instruments found in other aircraft. While this allows the pilot to have significantly more situational awareness of the battlefield, it takes time to get used to, and for inexperienced pilots, it can be easy to accidentally tap the wrong button on the screen.

After several moments of silence, the student realized that something was wrong and began troubleshooting the problem, thinking that his radio had failed. Because the F-35 is only a single-seat aircraft, as instructors, we need to monitor students from a separate F-35. As I flew formation off him, I noticed his altitude start to drift by several hundred feet—a telltale sign that he was beginning to become overwhelmed as he struggled to manage his cross-check.

Within thirty seconds, he found the mistake and switched over to the correct radio frequency. On the radio, though, I could hear that he had a slightly higher pitch in his voice, along with more pauses and faster breathing when he spoke. For the remainder of the flight, it was like I was with a completely different student—the collected, above-average student was now flying erratically. He began to miss radio calls while also failing to descend at the proper times during the recovery. He even tried to cut off another formation of fighters, requiring me to intervene several times.

In the debrief after the flight, we analyzed what had happened and found the root cause—he was angry with himself for making such a simple mistake. He was also afraid that he might have failed the flight, something he had never done before. The anger and fear had pushed him into a fight-or-flight response, which began to shut down his prefrontal cortex and

190 I THE ART OF CLEAR THINKING

therefore his ability to make logical decisions. The mistake had, within seconds, transformed an above-average student into one who struggled with even basic aircraft control.

After flying with hundreds of students over the years, I can say his experience isn't unique—new pilots, despite having performed well in pilot training, are prone to quickly mentally unraveling during a flight. Often, it's because they haven't learned to manage their emotions yet. They fear letting others or themselves down. The weight of expectations for fighter pilots can be heavy—there are thousands of people who have worked to enable you to complete your mission. There may have been spies on the ground who put their lives on the line to gather the intelligence, drone and satellite operators who spent weeks canvassing the area, tanker crews who launched from a different continent to refuel you, operations centers filled with people monitoring your real-time progress—all so that you can put your weapons on target. You're the last link in the chain, and if you make a mistake, everyone's effort is wasted. In many cases, these opportunities are fleeting, and the target may never again present itself.

In addition to the fear of failure, there is also the fear of injury or death. In low-threat battlefields like Afghanistan, the risk of being shot down isn't particularly high. We're usually at fifteen thousand feet and relatively safe. However, fighter aircraft must balance performance and reliability, often at the expense of each other. The modern F-16 crash rate is approximately two jets destroyed for every one hundred thousand flight hours. As a squadron, when we deployed, we were expecting to fly nearly ten thousand hours, meaning there was a one in five chance that one of us would crash. In the back of your mind, you're always aware that if your engine quits—or any other critical part of your aircraft fails—within minutes, you'll be evading in a hostile countryside, with everyone looking to capture you.

Less than a year prior to my unit arriving in Afghanistan, an F-16 was taking off from Bagram when the pilot saw a large explosion at the front of his aircraft. What followed was a loud, grinding sound along with two big thumps and significant vibrations. The jet was just twenty feet above the runway but already traveling 250 miles per hour—too fast to attempt a landing with the remaining runway. Feeling the loss of thrust, despite being in full afterburner, the pilot quickly zoomed his aircraft, trading airspeed for altitude, and pulled the ejection handle, triggering a complex sequence of events to save his life.

Initially, the canopy was explosively separated from the aircraft and blown clear of its flight path. A rocket motor inside the seat then fired, producing over four thousand pounds of thrust while hurtling him clear of the jet with nearly twenty times the force of gravity.[1] The seat then separated, and within two seconds from the time he pulled the handle, he was under a full parachute.

Ejecting from an aircraft is an extremely violent process that causes spine fractures in nearly a third of pilots. Once clear of the aircraft, the ordeal isn't over. The impact with the ground is also substantial, equivalent to jumping off the roof of a house with over fifty pounds of gear. An ejection can

---

1. Most pilots are two inches shorter in the aftermath of an ejection.

happen at any time, and because there's minimal control of the parachute, it's easy to land on boulders, trees, power lines, and other hazards that can cause further injuries. The danger in combat is that even a small injury, such as rolling an ankle, can be fatal when trying to evade the enemy. Fortunately, in this case, the pilot only sustained minor injuries, and amazingly, because he was so close to the base, he was able to run back to the gate before the Taliban or even friendly rescue forces could even be mobilized.

Unfortunately, most pilots aren't nearly as lucky. Fighter pilots are some of the few people who go deep behind enemy lines, where there's a significant chance of them being left alone. Although we'll usually go in as part of a larger package of fighters, the thin margins for fuel and logistics usually don't allow the other aircraft to remain overhead for more than just a few minutes. Also, in Afghanistan, because we only had two fighter aircraft airborne within the entire country at any given time, if multiple troops on the ground came under fire, we would often split, leaving each of us on our own and well out of radio range if we had to eject. In the high mountains, a helicopter rescue was unlikely, meaning we would be forced to evade for several days the Taliban and ISIS fighters, who would be doing everything in their power to find us. And if they did, recent history has shown that the outcome would be terrible.

Two years prior, a Jordanian pilot suffered a mechanical malfunction while flying over Syria. The pilot, Muath al-Kasassbeh, was twenty-seven and flying one of his first combat missions, which consisted of a joint strike with another squadron from my own base. Eventually, he was forced to eject from his damaged F-16; however, ISIS fighters were able to quickly capture him.

Muath was tortured for weeks during his captivity, and, after a failed negotiation with the Jordanian government, ISIS released a highly produced video across social media showing an injured Muath being immolated in a cage. At the end of the video, many of his fellow pilots' names were displayed— likely information gained through his torture, along with a bounty of $20,000 for each pilot killed.

The torture and killing of Muath al-Kasassbeh isn't unique—due to the strategic importance that a fighter aircraft can have on the battlefield, the symbolism of capturing its pilot and torturing them isn't lost on the enemy. Today's non-state actors don't follow the law of armed conflict, nor do they abide by the Geneva convention, which means that no mercy can be expected from the enemy. Because capture isn't a viable option in certain areas of the world, many fighter pilots that I've deployed with have made up their mind to take their own lives before falling into enemy hands.

A year after the killing of Muath al-Kasassbeh, another fighter aircraft, this one flown by Major Roman Filipov, was hit by a portable surface-to-air missile just 120 miles away from where Muath was captured. His aircraft subsequently caught fire, forcing him to eject. As he parachuted to the ground, the rebels continued firing at him. After landing, he radioed that he had ejected and was surrounded by the enemy. Filipov was last seen on live footage with a mob of rebels approaching him. Just before they reached him, Filipov could be heard yelling, "This one's for you, guys!" before detonating a grenade in his hands.

When in combat, there's always some element of fear. However, fear is manageable. Preparation and real-world experience can go a long way toward mitigating it; however, I've found that mental-toughness training is one of the most valuable and yet one of the most underutilized areas for dealing with strong emotions.

Back when I was going through pilot training, I wasn't exceptional at any particular aspect of flying. The one advantage I had was mental-toughness training. This came from my time at the Air Force Academy, where I was an intercollegiate boxer. What fascinated me about the sport was the unique combination of physical and mental skills that needed to be developed to win against an opponent. Though I had played sports all my life up to that point, none of them came close to the mental toughness required in boxing.

In boxing, you're alone in the ring with an opponent; there's no one else to help you. It's a combat sport where you're fighting another human who has been training to knock you out and hurt you in front of your friends and family. Though my physical skills were improving, I realized I wasn't as mentally prepared as I needed to be. The stress before fights led me to being fatigued by the time I climbed into the ring. During the fights themselves, the pressure often made it difficult to focus. When I made mistakes, I would dwell on them instead of focusing on my game plan. Sometimes I would get hit with a combination early in the fight, and the fear of getting knocked out would cause me to be less aggressive than I should have been. Other times, I would be cruising to victory and my mind would drift to what I was going to do after the fight, resulting in mistakes. At the time, I didn't realize that

I was mentally holding myself back; however, it was a chance encounter that changed my mindset and allowed me to gain much more control over my emotions.

The Air Force Academy is in Colorado Springs, which is also where the U.S. Olympic training center is located. One day, I was waiting outside the academy's human performance lab to take part in a study analyzing athletes in high-altitude environments. Because the Academy is located at over seven thousand feet above sea level, it provides a unique testing ground for altitude-based studies. Sitting next to me was a sports psychologist from the Olympic training center. We started talking about mental-performance training and how nearly every Olympic athlete had a dedicated mental workout plan to go along with their physical workouts.

As I learned more about the field, I began to understand that what I was experiencing during the fights was my body's natural response to stress and pressure. More importantly, there were best practices that I could apply to overcome them, such as visualization, self-talk, and specialized breath techniques. To go along with my physical preparation, I began mentally training for fights and noticed that my boxing improved, particularly when the stakes were high. I also enjoyed the fights more, which led to me dedicating more time to training, further enhancing my performance. However, the real breakthrough happened when I started applying the training to my life outside the ring.

I began to use the techniques for important tests or when I had to speak in front of a large group. I used them when I went skydiving and when I flew a glider for the first time. Without a doubt, they improved my performance while also reducing my stress. While they weren't 100 percent effective, they gave me a plan for managing my mindset and emotions. They weren't a replacement for hard work and preparation, but it felt as if I had unlocked a significant increase in performance.

By the time I attended pilot training several years later, I expected to hear about how these techniques could be implemented from a pilot's perspective. While the instruction was world-class, there wasn't any time spent on how to handle emotions or how they affect the decisions we make. I realized that the mindset training that I had been practicing over the last several years gave me a huge advantage. Although I wasn't the most talented pilot, I could lock in when I needed to, and when I made a mistake flying, I didn't let it unravel me.

Mentally, that's where many students struggled. Pilot training is one of the most competitive, fast-paced programs in the world. Only 3 percent of applicants are selected to even begin the training. Most students have excelled at everything in their lives up to that point. However, each class consisted of thirty students competing for just a few fighter spots. On my first day of training, the base commander came into our classroom and after a brief talk told us to close our eyes. He said, "Raise your hand if you want to fly a fighter." He then told us to open our eyes. All thirty students had their hands raised. He said, "Two of you will get a fighter slot; the rest of you will fly transports and tankers. Think about that while you're here." With that, he walked out, and the training began.

Early on, it seemed that those who had flown extensively in the civilian world would easily receive the fighter slots. One student had already been a commercial pilot before joining the Air Force and had logged thousands of hours flying by this point. However, as the training progressed, the amount of overlap with civilian flying grew smaller and smaller. There came a point when everyone in the class, regardless of their experience, was pushed beyond their limit and failed either a maneuver or an entire flight.

For some students, a small mistake would quickly spiral out of control. They couldn't regulate their emotions, and the fear of failure would overwhelm them. One of the students, who was doing reasonably well, imploded over the course of a week—failing three consecutive rides and washing out of the course before the weekend. Even the commercial pilot, despite cruising through the first half of the training, only graduated in the middle of the pack due to his inability to stay resilient after making mistakes. Even though I wasn't exceptional during any phase of the training, when I did fail, I was able to quickly bounce back, in large part due to the mental tools I had learned while boxing.

For the next several years, I continued to practice the mental training, which helped me considerably. As I progressed into a leadership role, I passed along the mindset to the younger pilots; however, there still wasn't anything being formally taught. It wasn't until I transitioned to the F-35—where I met a three-star general who oversaw all of the Air Force's flight training, consisting of 60,000 personnel and 1,600 aircraft—that things began to change.

At the time, tactical training for the F-35 was brand-new—up to that point, pilots were primarily gathering data points to aid in the development of the aircraft. However, the F-35 was soon to become operational, and senior military leaders were interested in how they could maximize the training for future pilots. The general and I spoke about how the mental-performance side was still significantly underutilized. He was in the process of revamping pilot training and wanted to not only streamline the flight training but to optimize the entire weapon system, including the pilot. Mental-performance training aligned closely with his goals.

Change can be difficult for an organization the size of the Air Force. There are so many internal and external groups fighting over limited resources that many ideas never make it out of the planning phase. Dedicated mental training was also a significant change in culture—up to that point, the belief had been that the mental side was innate. If a student unraveled under pressure, then they didn't have what it took to become a fighter pilot. It was known as an *eat-your-own mentality*, where poorly performing students were quickly washed out of the training. However, the general, along with the heroic work by a single flight doctor, was able to secure a grant to test the idea of mental-performance training at the base where I was stationed. The idea was that we spent tens of millions of dollars training each pilot, but almost nothing on optimizing their minds and bodies. What if we built a syllabus using the latest performance techniques to strengthen every fighter pilot's mind and body to optimize their decision-making ability?

AFGHANISTAN

After the controller said, "It's bad. . . . It's not looking good for him," the radio went silent. I could feel a pit in my stomach and a numb sensation wash over me. I couldn't help but think about the soldier's family and how they would soon be receiving a knock on the door. When they answered, there would be an officer and chaplain, both dressed in their formal uniforms, waiting to give them the news about their husband's or son's death. For several seconds, I was immersed in the thought of the soldier and his family.

The logical side of my brain knew I had to regain focus on the tactical situation, but my emotions lagged. I tried to push the thoughts out of my mind, but they kept coming back. I began mechanically going through several of the techniques that I had learned almost a decade earlier. Slowly, I was able to refocus on the situation unfolding.

A new enemy sniper position began opening fire on the team. Coordinating with the controller, I had my wingman drop a five-hundred-pound bomb on the position. A minute later, the airburst smart bomb detonated, disintegrating the building in a cloud of smoke and dust over the area. The AC-130's radios were still down. With no link to the outside world, they couldn't verify their targets.

Close air support is difficult even in the best of conditions because it requires detailed integration between the troops on the ground and the aircraft above them. Objects can look entirely different from the air, particularly when viewed through a black-and-white targeting pod. Think back to the last time you took a flight and looked down on a city—it's often difficult to even make out key landmarks. Now imagine doing that in a foreign country above sprawling villages with an enemy that's intermixed with the friendly forces. If you drop a bomb too far away from the enemy, it'll have a minimal effect on them; if you drop it too close to the friendly forces, it can kill the very people you're trying to protect.

The AC-130, despite not having a working radio, began to lay down a constant stream of fire into the field where they had last seen the enemy. It was a bold move by the crew to protect the troops, going against regulations and putting their careers on the line. Through my targeting pod, I could see the rounds exploding and ricocheting throughout the field. Outside of my canopy, I could see the full effect from the AC-130 as it turned the area into a hellish landscape of rubble and smoke, causing a group of the enemy fighters to flee.

Other fighters, however, had spread out into the town. They now occupied several buildings and were engaging the friendly forces from multiple directions. The troops were relying on my wingman and me to clear a path out of the town. However, the AC-130 was still in a tight orbit, preventing us from having a clear path of fire to the enemy. In addition, because of the configuration of our sensors, we were forced to orbit in the opposite direction, meaning we would have to thread the needle and drop our bombs through the AC-130's orbit while also hitting moving targets on the ground, a complex attack that left little room for error.

With my wingman closely trailing me, I accelerated to just under the speed of sound and widened our orbit to give the AC-130 time to circle back. Once the large aircraft banked toward us, I rolled in on the target and waited for the AC-130 to cross my nose. As the aircraft tracked through the front of my heads-up display, it was time to release my bomb, an uncomfortable feeling with the crew of thirteen directly in front of me. I pushed down on the weapons-release button and a moment later felt a jolt as the bomb released from my wing. As it arced through the air, I checked back into my orbit and began guiding it through my targeting pod onto the moving enemy. Thirty seconds later, my bomb impacted, followed in quick succession by my wingman's bomb. "One's splash," I said over the radio, indicating my weapon had detonated. "Two's splash," my wingman followed.

"Good hits, good hits!" the controller said as we continued to search for additional targets. By this point, the AC-130 was now "Winchester," meaning it was out of ammo and returning to base. It was an impressive show of force by the crew. They had done everything they could, even overheating their weapons, in order to keep the enemy at bay.

The troops on the ground had been in a sustained firefight for several hours and were now running low on ammo and supplies. My formation was also low on weapons; my wingman was down to just three small laser rockets, and I was down to my last weapon—a giant two-thousand-pound bomb designed to destroy caves. I radioed back to headquarters via satcom that we needed additional aircraft—without more support, the troops would be stranded in the town while the ISIS fighters reinforced their positions. The response I received was that there weren't any aircraft available for the next two hours but that the Army was working on coordinating a long-range missile salvo onto the enemy's location.

To maintain continuous coverage over the troops, I sent my wingman off to refuel from the orbiting tanker. By minimizing my fuel burn rate, I could stay on station until he made it back. By now, the ISIS fighters had consolidated into a single compound directly across from the troops, with only a dry ravine separating them. The walls around the compound were giving the enemy both the high ground and protection while they continued to fire at the troops. It would need to be destroyed; however, I was now the only aircraft on station and down to my last weapon—the cave-busting two-thousand-pound bomb. Dropping it on the compound would put the troops well within the lethal blast radius of the bomb. It was a danger-close drop, which meant there was a chance of wounding or killing the friendly troops. Though I had dropped many danger-close weapons in combat, this was incredibly close—nearly three times closer than the recommended range.

The force of a bomb exploding doesn't dissipate linearly—it adheres to a strong long-tail power law, meaning one-third of the distance wouldn't subject the troops to just three times the force but *twenty-seven times* the blast force, overpressure, and fragmentation of a bomb dropped at the outer edge of what was considered danger-close. Over one thousand pounds of shrapnel would be released into the air, traveling at hypersonic speeds of up to five thousand miles per hour—fast enough for a steel BB to penetrate over an inch of armored steel. The rapid overpressure followed by the vacuum left behind would cause additional significant damage. In training, we had never even simulated dropping a bomb this close to friendly troops—it was automatically assumed it would cause a fratricide.

This wasn't a normal situation, though. The troops were pinned down by accurate gunfire from a fortified compound. We didn't have much time—they were running low on ammo, and I would soon be at my bingo fuel. There were two options that I could think of that would mitigate the force of the bomb. The first was to drop it on the opposite side of the compound to where the friendly forces were, thereby shielding them with the compound itself. However, this was my last bomb—I had to make sure it destroyed the enemy position. The other option was to quickly reprogram the fuse so that it delayed the detonation for a split second after it impacted the target. This would cause the bomb to go off several feet underground, reducing the blast and fragmentation.

I would be held responsible for any weapons my wingman and I dropped. Knowingly dropping a two-thousand-pound bomb that close to troops went against all our tactical regulations—if any of the troops were injured or killed, there was a strong chance I would never fly again. There was a possibility that I could even be court-martialed. However, one of the best parts about combat is that most people don't care about their careers—they do what they need to do to accomplish the mission and bring people home alive. I've seen tanker crews fly well below their bingo fuel to refuel other aircraft, I've seen pilots take off below weather minimums to help troops under fire, and I've seen people employ weapons outside their recommended envelope because that's the only way they could save the troops on the ground. The rules and regulations were designed for a generic scenario—combat puts people in situations with a combination of variables that could have never been forecasted ahead of time.

The only thing that mattered to me was finding the best option that would maximize the upside while minimizing the downside to the troops on the ground. Being detached at fifteen thousand feet above the battlefield, I could see the big picture. The enemy was reinforcing their position and only getting stronger while the troops were being ground down. There wasn't any way to know how it would play out; however, I estimated that if I did nothing, there was at least a 50 percent chance of them taking additional casualties. There was also a small but growing chance that ISIS reinforcements would reach a tipping point, allowing them to overrun the troops.

To find the value of dropping the bomb, I used a chart that I had memorized before the deployment called the *probability of incapacitation*. In the chart, there were different ranges for the various weapons we carried, along with the probability of injuring someone at those ranges. However, the drop today was well off the charts; I would need to extrapolate the risk. Accounting for the power law, I estimated there was a 30 percent chance of injuring the troops if they weren't behind any cover. I could likely lower it to around 10 percent by setting the fuse to explode underground. I could further lower it to likely just a few percent if the troops were able to get behind substantial cover, like large rocks or a dirt mound.

I relayed to the controller that I could destroy the compound but that it posed a significant risk to them—they would need to be behind cover when the bomb went off, covering their ears and opening their mouths to prevent their eardrums and lungs from rupturing from the overpressure. Conferring with his commander on the ground, they agreed that the risk was worth it.

With that, I pushed the throttle forward and accelerated to give the bomb the most amount of energy to maneuver to the target. I then rolled in, feeling the g's push me into the seat, and lined up the steering bar in my heads-up display. From there, I looked down into my avionics and adjusted my aim point in the targeting pod so that it was slightly offset and away from the friendly troops but still on the compound roof. I pulled halfway back on the trigger to fire the laser, passing weapons-quality targeting coordinates into the bomb. I double-checked I was in master arm hot and then hammered down on the red weapons-release button. For a second and a half, nothing happened as the signal made its way to the bomb and the clamps released. Though I've dropped many bombs over my career, that second and a half always feels like it takes forever, particularly when it's an important attack. Eventually, the car-size weapon separated from my wing, causing the jet to roll in the opposite direction. Over the radio, I called, "Weapon away. Impact in forty-five seconds."

At this point, there was nothing more I could do—the bomb was now past the point of no return and on its own. Though modern weapons are incredibly precise and highly reliable, there are still dozens of failure points that can cause the bomb to miss its intended mark. In the previous month, my squadron had dropped several bombs that went "dumb," as we call it, completely missing the target due to a failure within the bomb. With the friendly troops so close, there was no margin for error on this drop.

As the bomb arced toward the target, I checked back into my orbit. My targeting pod was zoomed in and fixed on the compound. I could see the hot muzzle flashes of the ISIS fighters as the time to impact continued to count down. "Ten seconds," I warned over the radio. The giant bomb was now traveling just under the speed of sound and making the noise of a freight train as it flew toward the target. Because it was traveling so fast, it wouldn't be heard until just seconds before impact. As the countdown hit zero, I could see the bomb streak across my screen and impact the back side of the compound. A shock wave quickly propagated outward before the entire screen washed out from the heat generated by the bomb. The white heat was soon replaced by a thick cloud mushrooming up from where the compound had just been.

This was the moment of truth—the bomb had hit its intended target, but had I killed or incapacitated any of the friendly troops? I had knowingly dropped a bomb well within the danger-close range of the weapon and put the troops' lives at risk. I believed that the risk had been worth it; however, with only thirty seconds to make the decision, had I missed something? If I had, I would have to live with that for the rest of my life, with the knowledge that I had mistakenly killed or maimed the troops I was protecting. Would I lose my wings or be court-martialed? I could see negative thoughts forming in my mind and distracting me from the current situation. I went back to my mental training and was able to let the thoughts go. There would be plenty of time after the mission to think about those things—right now, I was still making a difference on the battlefield and needed to focus on the next decision.

Ten slow seconds of silence went by. The smoke above the target had now dissipated enough so that I could see through it—there was nothing left but rubble and blowing trash. I was about to key the mic to ask the status of the troops when the controller came back with, "Good hit, good hit! We're all good!" In the background, I heard someone yell out, "Holy sh*t!" while several more were hollering.

The compound had been the enemy's primary stronghold. With it gone, many of the remaining fighters pulled back into tall grass and trees near the riverbank. By this point, my wingman had finally made it back from the tanker, topped off with a full load of fuel. After a quick status report to update his situational awareness, I started making my way toward the tanker.

The sun was beginning to set, the mountain peaks, many over twenty thousand feet, were creating long shadows across the valleys. While en route, I called back to headquarters to get an update—the Army had approved a large rocket strike that would occur in the next thirty minutes. Now that it was getting dark, I took off my helmet and disconnected the augmented reality visor, replacing it with my night vision goggle bracket. Looking out the cockpit, I could see how desolate the environment was—traveling only a few thousand feet over the peaks, I could see the wind spraying the snow off the bare mountains.

After joining up with the tanker and refueling, it was now dark. Looking through my night vision goggles, everything was now shades of green and black. Though the sun had fully set, I could still see the remnants of the horizon glowing light green. After several minutes, I rejoined my wingman and got back into the fight. ISIS fighters were now moving through the brush, attempting to flank the friendly troops. Over satcom, headquarters informed me to keep a wide orbit; the rocket salvo would be commencing soon and they wanted to make sure that they didn't inadvertently shoot us down, which was a welcome warning.

Thirty seconds later, the rockets began launching from the Jalalabad air base, known as J-Bad. Although it was dozens of miles away, my night vision goggles washed out in bright green as the rockets were launched. I could see each bright orb of light flying high into the atmosphere. Typically, only one or two were launched at a time; however, I counted over a dozen launched in quick succession. As the last rocket motor burned out, there was an eerie calm as the warheads arced over one hundred thousand feet directly above us.

Minutes later, I could see the warheads fly between my wingman and me—they were traveling so fast that they just appeared to be long streaks of light. They began impacting the field in a grid pattern, each one several hundred feet from the previous strike. The Army, not knowing precisely where the ISIS fighters were, had decided to destroy the *entire* area. After several seconds, it lay smoldering with small fires burning. For the next hour, we stayed on station while the troops made it back to their forward operating base.

MENTAL TRAINING

The experiences I gained in combat helped to shape the training that we developed to enhance the mental toughness of fighter pilots. With the general's approval along with funding, we now had a rare opportunity to implement the training across the base. There was much more at stake, though—our base would be used as an experiment, and if the program was successful, it would be implemented throughout *all* the pilot training bases in the U.S. Air Force. That meant that every new pilot would, from the start, be given guidance and tools for how to manage their emotions so that they could maintain peak mental performance both inside and outside of the cockpit.

As instructors developing the program, we wanted to give pilots tools that could be used across a wide range of experiences. Although they would be critical when they were making life-and-death decisions, we also wanted them to be useful for day-to-day experiences. When leading, speaking, or receiving feedback, we wanted them to be able to seamlessly regulate their mindset so that they could maintain optimal performance. We also wanted them to be able to use the skills outside of work.

High performance isn't something that can be turned on and off—to thrive in the cockpit, the pilots needed to thrive in their personal lives. A military lifestyle comes with a lot of added stress. On average, fighter pilots are gone over half the time and are expected to move to a new base every three years. These moves are often to austere locations on the other side of the world and can come with minimal notice. We wanted to give the pilots tools to regulate their emotions so that they could make the best possible decisions for themselves and their families.

Over the next year, we developed a first-of-its-kind program that all new pilots learning to fly the F-16 or F-35 would receive throughout their training. Unlike previous generations that were expected to find a way to be mentally tough on their own—a sink-or-swim mentality—we treated it as a skill that could be learned and improved. Although some pilots were predisposed to handle emotions better than others, everyone had the ability to get better. From the first day the students arrived, they would be training their minds and bodies in addition to learning to fly the aircraft.

The strength of the program was that it merged fighter pilot wisdom that has been accumulated since the early days of aviation with modern cognitive-performance research. This gave us a blended approach, where we could identify concepts that overlapped, giving us a higher degree of confidence of which principles were effective. The formalized syllabus then ensured that all students received the necessary training. Overall, it consisted of several pillars:

1. The first concept was that you don't rise to the level of your expectations but rather fall to the level of your preparation. It's not enough to just understand the concept of mental toughness; it needs to be practiced until it's a subconscious reflex. As stress and pressure rise, it's easy to become consumed with emotions and lose the ability to logically make decisions. That's why you lose twenty IQ points as soon as you put on your helmet. The same is true when speaking in front of large groups of people, interviewing for a job, or any other high-pressure situation. Only by practicing a skill thousands of times are you able to rely on it when it matters most.

   While mental-toughness training is an important aspect of high performance, it's not a substitute for learning the underlying skill. When flying, speaking, or playing a sport, no amount of mental-toughness training will make up for a lack of preparation in the execution. The training should be repeated until many of the skills and decisions become routine.

For the student pilots, that meant using simulators to practice the same maneuvers repeatedly until they were deeply ingrained within their mental framework. We then increased the difficulty and practiced the maneuvers in the air, where they were subjected to both the physical stress of high g's and the mental stress from poor weather, traffic, malfunctions, and other unscripted events. Finally, we would incorporate the maneuvers into large force exercises, where dozens of other aircraft and pilots would be counting on them to execute. By the end of the training, the students would have practiced the maneuvers over and over to the point where they were automatic—even during high-stress situations, they could fall back on the repetitions and have the confidence to know that they could successfully accomplish the given task.

2. The next concept was focus-based training. Our brains are incredibly powerful; however, much of the brain's effort is wasted on thinking about what's already happened or worrying about future events that we have no control over. The key to maximizing our mental resources is to focus only on what we have control over, which is the next decision to make.

No matter the level of execution, mistakes will always be made. Instead of spending mental bandwidth dwelling on them, it's important to let go of the thoughts and refocus on the current situation. There's a time for analyzing mistakes, and that's after the execution, during the debrief. Thinking about past mistakes while executing occupies attention that's better allocated toward something we have control over. The same is true about thinking too far into the future—it's a distraction that takes focus away from what's currently happening. Worrying about step 857 when you're only on step 15 is just a distraction. There are so many things that can go wrong and so much of it is out of our control that the best use of energy and time is focusing on the next decision while being flexible when things change.

Although it's difficult to control the thoughts we focus on, just like any other skill, with practice it becomes easier. While our goal was to enable pilots to use the training under extreme conditions, we started at the other end of the spectrum—alone in a quiet room using a type of meditation called *focus-based training.*

New pilots were given a training regimen like a physical workout plan. Initially, they just had to close their eyes for several minutes and be aware of the stream of thoughts that continually passed through their minds. Their only goal was to objectively watch the thoughts and not get fixated on any of them. When they noticed they had lost focus, they simply had to return to the objective state. Over time, the sessions would increase in length and the points of focus would change. We found that thirty minutes proved to be the optimal time between managing their busy schedules and continuing to improve.

Once the pilots were proficient in a quiet room, elements of the training were then introduced during workouts to increase the complexity and add physical stress. Eventually the training progressed into using the techniques in the simulator and then finally during flights.

3. One of the most important skills to learn is how to calm the body and mind down during stressful events. Even when flying straight and level, a fighter pilot's heart rate is often more than 100 beats per minute. During highly stressful periods or when pulling high amounts of g's, it's not uncommon for heart rates to eclipse 180 beats per minute, equivalent to an all-out sprint. At that heart rate, fine motor skills rapidly deteriorate, which are critical when flying a fighter aircraft—even a slight movement of the stick can cause an abrupt change in the direction of the aircraft, which can be catastrophic when dogfighting or refueling from a tanker.

The best way to calm the body and mind down is to focus on breathing. Breathing is one of the few processes of the body that's under both conscious and unconscious control. We don't need to think about it to breathe; however, unlike many automatic processes, such as digestion, we can also consciously take over and control it. As we experience fear and stress, our bodies shift into fight-or-flight mode, and our breathing becomes shallow and rapid. However, we can counteract it by consciously slowing down and deepening our breathing through our nose. This activates the parasympathetic nervous system, which can return the body to a more relaxed physical state and shift our decision-making back to the neocortex.

In the heat of the moment, it can be difficult to recognize your breathing rate. We often experience temporal distortion and have difficulty estimating how much time has elapsed. To help the students to assess their breathing rates, we had them silently count while they breathed. In one exercise, the students would practice what's called *box breathing*, whereby they would inhale for five seconds, hold for five seconds, exhale for five seconds, hold for five seconds, and continue doing this for five minutes. Another variation was called *triangle breathing*, where they would inhale for five seconds, exhale for five seconds, and then hold for five seconds before repeating the process. Although there are many different techniques, it ultimately came down to individual preference coupled with their body's oxygen demands. If you're running, swimming, or dogfighting, your body will need a far greater supply of oxygen than when you're less active. What's important isn't following a specific breathing pattern but learning how to slow down and deepen your breathing so that the mind can return to an optimum state as quickly as possible. It's also important that the breathing be done primarily through the nose as it optimizes the temperature, moisture, quantity, and circulation of the air better than the mouth. After having the students practice the focus-based breathing in a static environment, we then incorporated it into their physical workouts. This allowed them to use the techniques they had learned in a more dynamic environment, which served as a bridge between practicing the techniques in a quiet room and utilizing them while flying.

4. The next concept we incorporated was systematically building confidence. To sit on top of an engine producing over forty thousand pounds of thrust while hundreds of people on the battlefield are counting on you requires confidence. Without the confidence to make sound decisions, you're putting yourself and others at risk. This is part of the fighter pilots' ethos that goes back nearly a century. In the past, it was thought that either you had confidence or you didn't—and those who didn't were quickly weeded out. However, confidence is a skill that can be improved, primarily through our internal dialogue—how we talk to ourselves. Many of the students were perfectionists—high performers who put unnecessary pressure on themselves to succeed. This compounded the effects of stress during the decision-making process and would often cause them to fail at tasks they already knew how to perform. The extreme competition of pilot training coupled with the high standards expected of them during fighter training left many of them doubting their abilities and choking when it mattered most.

Many of the students berated themselves and had a negative internal dialogue. Although this could be a powerful motivator, it also created self-doubt, which was detrimental to making high-stakes decisions. The solution was to couple the focus training with a technique called *reframing*. Anytime they noticed an undermining thought, they needed to identify it and then replace it with a counterexample from their past. It was easier said than done—it had to be practiced to the point where it became habitual. We started slowly, by just spending a few minutes each day dedicated toward practicing the technique. We then incorporated it into workouts, then simulator sessions, and finally while flying.

5. We also implemented a type of visualization training known as *chair flying*. The technique dated back to World War II aviators; however, we made slight alterations based on modern neuroscience. Students would close their eyes and mentally rehearse a flight while incorporating as many senses as possible. This allowed them to practice the concepts they had learned in the same way they would be using them during an actual flight. While it was a great tool for preparation, we also used it to build their confidence. When chair flying, students would visualize themselves successfully completing each maneuver—if doubt crept in or they felt they had made a mistake, then they would simply repeat the maneuver or procedure until they had successfully completed it in their minds.

Over the course of the year, we tracked how the students did relative to historical data. We found that emotional regulation can be significantly improved by treating it as a skill. Everyone had the ability to get better. It soon became just one part of the many facets required to perform well as a fighter pilot. Overall, the washout rate decreased, and while the top students continued to do well, the average and below-average students made considerable gains in their performance. As instructors, we noticed that there was less of a snowball effect when a student made a mistake—they were able to keep their focus and carry on with the flight despite the setback.

The results were significant enough that the mental training was permanently implemented across *all* the pilot training bases in the Air Force. Students are now exposed to the techniques immediately so that by the time they begin flying fighters, they already have a foundation of mental toughness that they can further build upon. The training has been so effective that many other career fields throughout the Department of Defense—both war fighters on the front lines and support personnel out of harm's way—have implemented the techniques so that they can maintain peak mental performance.

7

PRIORITIZE AND BE DECISIVE

On November 12, 2016, a man named Ahmad Nayeb intentionally missed the early-morning bus out of Bagram Air Base, Afghanistan. Instead of getting on the bus, he began walking down the dark road in the predawn hours, illuminated every few hundred feet by diesel-generated light towers.

Ahmad was an Afghan native who was employed as a civilian contractor for Bagram Air Base, the largest international base in Afghanistan. Despite the drawdown that had seen U.S. forces in the country fall to fewer than 8,500 troops, Bagram still employed tens of thousands of civilians to augment its support functions. Instead of a base, Bagram would be better described as a fortified city. The continuous influx of supplies over the last fifteen years had turned the base into a sprawling sea of buildings and clamshell tents, all protected by gray concrete walls that stretched high into the air to protect the inhabitants from the daily mortar fire. During the day, the roads turned into a congested parade of buses, trucks, and construction machinery, while large armored vehicles circulated among them. Outside of the military, few of the inhabitants were from the United States—most were from other countries, such as India, Uganda, Ukraine, Kyrgyzstan, and Nepal, as well as from the surrounding Afghan countryside.

Ahmad was a self-admitted former Taliban member; however, after going through a reintegration program designed to "renounce violence via honorable means and live within the laws of Afghanistan," he was hired through a subcontractor to the Fluor Corporation, the largest engineering and construction company in the United States—the same company that had quietly overseen such megaprojects as the rebuilding of Iraq, the Hurricane Katrina recovery, and the building of the Trans-Alaska Pipeline System.

For the next five years, Ahmad worked throughout the base's vehicle yard doing low-level maintenance, eventually migrating to the hazardous material section of the depot, where he became the only employee working throughout the night. Strangely, Ahmad didn't have a direct supervisor—depending on the job he was doing that day, Ahmad would get sporadic supervision and then would be left on his own. While he never had any formal counseling or disciplinary action, he was repeatedly caught sleeping and would disappear for hours at a time. As another employee later said, "It was normal for him not to be in the work area."

As a hazardous materials worker, Ahmad wasn't required or authorized to check out tools; however, in the previous months, he had successfully checked out a multimeter—a tool used to measure voltage, current, and resistance—*nine* times. When questioned by a supervisor about the repeated use of unauthorized tools, he had said he was fixing a radio on one occasion and hair clippers on another. Ahmad, however, was building a suicide vest, and the vehicle yard was the perfect area on base to build one—he had access to nearly everything he needed, such as wires, triggering switches, tools, and, most importantly, unsupervised time. The only thing he didn't have access to were explosives, though he was able to slowly accumulate enough by smuggling a small amount each day onto the base through a hidden compartment in his tobacco bag.

And so, on the morning of November 12, Ahmad left the vehicle yard for the final time. In theory, there should have been one last system in place to detect his absence—Ahmad was scheduled to leave on the 4:45 a.m. bus, which would have taken him to the main gate. Bagram policy required local Afghans to be escorted and in constant view of their supervisors; however, Fluor's supervisors were replaced or changed out on a near-weekly basis, leaving them reliant on a self-sign-in sheet to maintain accountability. Local workers were left behind so frequently that a second bus often needed to be dispatched to pick up the stragglers.

Ahmad had chosen November 12 for a reason. Normally, operations at Bagram were conducted around the clock—there weren't any breaks from the operation tempo, regardless of whether it was the night or weekend. However, for a few select holidays throughout the year, the base's leadership allowed small gatherings to help the morale of the troops. November 12 was one of those days—it was the observance of Veterans Day, and, to celebrate it, a five-kilometer run was scheduled to begin at 6:15 a.m., just as the sun was beginning to rise.

For the next fifty-three minutes, Ahmad walked alone down the main avenue, named Disney Drive, and toward the base's headquarters, which served as the starting point for the race. Hundreds of people had already gathered in the predawn chill in anticipation of the race—each dressed in their standard-issue workout uniform for their respective units. Ahmad began silently passing through the outer layers of the crowd. Three hundred meters from the assembly point, a twenty-year-old Army specialist, Winston Hencely, noticed Ahmad and thought he looked out of place. Hencely repeatedly told Ahmad to stop; however, his requests went unanswered, causing Ahmad to speed up his pace as he pushed his way through the crowd. Hencely ran up and grabbed Ahmad's shoulder, and it was then that he felt the bulky explosive vest under Ahmad's robe. Before he had time to yell out, Ahmad pressed the detonator, exploding the vest and sending hundreds of nuts and bolts ripping throughout the crowd.

Across the runway were my barracks. I had flown a mission the night before and had just gone to bed when I heard the blast. At first, I didn't think anything of it—Bagram was the modern-day Wild West. At any given hour, there were outgoing missile launches, incoming mortar fire, and base cannons shooting into the air. When walking outside, it wasn't uncommon to see dark smoke billowing from a section of the base for no apparent reason. There was so much going on, and we were so busy, that it all became normal—if it didn't affect you, you didn't worry about it.

With that in mind, I went back to sleep. Sometime later, I heard the base's loudspeakers go off with a cavalry charge horn—the signal that the base was under attack. I got out of bed just in time for another pilot to walk in, telling me that it was an internal attack with several dead and already over a dozen wounded. He had been in contact with our senior leadership, and my orders were to go back to sleep and be ready to fly an F-16 that afternoon once the base was ready to launch aircraft.

Trying to go back to sleep after hearing the base was under attack with multiple casualties was difficult. However, the Air Force has done multiple studies over the years, analyzing the length and quality of sleep versus pilots' performance and shown that sleep is one of the most important factors in preparing for a flight. With that in mind, I tried to sleep with some success; however, it mostly consisted of me resting while thinking about what the afternoon would bring. Although we were issued sleeping pills known as *no gos*, I wanted to be alert enough to defend the barracks in case it was directly attacked.

After several hours, I got up and looked out the window and was shocked at how the base had changed. Just hours earlier, buses, trucks, pedestrians, and armored vehicles were all jockeying for position through the narrow dirt roads of the base. Now there wasn't a single person in sight. Everything was completely shut down. All aircraft, even our F-16s, had been grounded, making the base silent for the first time in years.

In the hours following the suicide blast, an overwhelming amount of information began pouring in. Perimeter guards reported unmanned aerial systems flying above the base, additional suspected improvised explosive devices had been found, and suspicious crowds were now gathering at the entry-control points around the base. Small-arms fire as well as other unconfirmed explosions had also been reported. It appeared that the base was set to come under a large and complex attack, so it was decided that our squadron needed to launch F-16s to defend the base. I was told that I would be leading two F-16s that evening for one of the first launches since the blast.

The base was at its highest alert posture, meaning everyone was locked down and ordered not to move while keeping their firearms on them. Anyone stepping outside would need full "battle rattle," as it's called, meaning that in addition to our weapons, we would need our bulletproof vests with ceramic plates, as well as our Kevlar helmets. With the threat of a chemical attack, we also carried our chem masks, attached to our waists for quick access.

As our showtime grew near, my wingman and I met up at the end of the barracks in our bulky gear. We then began the silent walk toward the flight line, where our operations building was located. As the sun set, wind ripped through the gravel roads, sending talcum-like dust into the air, creating a dark red hue. A city that, just the night before, had thousands of people driving and walking through the streets was now empty. There weren't even security personnel. We later found out that in the postattack chaos, many had deemed themselves nonessential and had stayed sheltered indoors.

Entering the operations building, my wingman and I received an intelligence brief with a more detailed picture of what had happened to the base as well as what to expect from the enemy. We were told that the deadliest action they might take would be a vehicle-borne improvised explosive device penetrating the base, which our job would be to stop at all costs. Afterward, I briefed my wingman on the mission and that, because of the security threat, if one of us had to ground abort, the other needed to take off, going against our standard procedure of working as a team—we would accept increased risk to defend the base. We then put on our flight gear, which consisted of our harness to tie us into the ejection seat, our G suit, our survival vest, and handgun. Because of the heightened security posture and the threat of enemy snipers in the area, we then put on our Kevlar vests and helmets, bringing the gear to over fifty pounds.

Stepping out of the fortified building into the night, we were again greeted by the cold wind, which numbed our faces as we walked through the darkness toward our aircraft. The F-16s then came into view—the overhead floodlights bathed the jets in a white fluorescent light. Normally, there were dozens of maintainers preparing the jets for launch—this time, though, there was no one in sight. The ramp was silent except for an electric buzz from the security lights.

Walking up to my jet, I saw a single crew chief, who looked like a teenager, standing next to it. His bulletproof vest and helmet were both overly large for his small frame. In his hands was an M16 rifle, which, when he saw me walking up, he slung over his shoulder so that we could salute and shake hands. I asked him where everybody was. He said that everyone else had been ordered inside, and he been out there alone for the last half an hour, waiting.

As a career field, maintainers are some of the hardest-working people in the Air Force. Fighter aircraft require over a dozen hours of maintenance for every hour they fly. It's the maintainers who work throughout the night, crawling on their hands and knees in the engine intake to make sure that the planes are ready to fly. A teenage crew chief, standing by himself in the cold night, is a perfect example of their mentality.

After doing the walk-around inspection of the jet, I climbed up the ladder and into the cockpit. I gave a final handshake to the crew chief and began turning on the avionics. I signaled to him that I was starting the engine and flipped the switch to activate the jet-fuel starter. As compressed air began slowly rotating the engine, I lowered the canopy and continued to bring the jet's engine and mission systems to life. It was then that out of the corner of my eye I caught something large moving.

After a few seconds, I realized it was a fuel truck speeding toward me, only it wasn't a U.S. one—instead of the standard olive-green ones used throughout the base, it was a faded yellow and covered in dirt. The truck was traveling faster than normal as it weaved its way around the barricades toward us. I could see the suspension loading up as it sped past the revetments where other F-16s were parked. As it drew closer, I could make out large foreign lettering across the side of the truck above its rusted-out fenders.

A large vehicle-borne improvised explosive device was the single biggest threat to U.S. forces in Afghanistan. The massive size of the explosion could rip through nearly all fortifications. It was a threat that didn't even need approval to attack. If we were able to confirm that we had found one, we had full authority to destroy it, regardless of the collateral damage it would cause. Two months prior, one had detonated in Kabul, the capital of Afghanistan, just to the south of our base. After first responders arrived, a second one detonated, dramatically increasing the death toll. Just two days prior in another attack, a group of terrorists had rammed the German consulate in Mazar-i-Sharif with a truck filled with explosives. The attack caused over 120 casualties and had severely damaged the infrastructure.

Our squadron's twelve F-16s represented the entire fighter force in Afghanistan. We had been briefed multiple times that we were a strategic target for the Taliban and to be on the lookout for sabotage and other attempts to destroy our aircraft. The truck barreling toward me fit the description.

There have been a handful of times during my career where I thought there was a chance that I might die. Usually, it's been a near reflex when multiple jets have passed next to each other with supersonic closing speeds. The event usually lasts just a few seconds. All background thoughts disappear as the mind focuses on the best way to solve the problem. In this case, however, there was plenty of time. It wasn't a reflexive decision but rather a methodical one to make—there was an understanding that despite the uncertainty, I would need to act decisively.

OVERLORD

An hour and a half's drive south of London, there's a home sitting on the English countryside overlooking Portsmouth

Harbour. Known as Southwick House, it today looks like an unassuming bed-and-breakfast among the surrounding trees and farmland. Though quiet and museum-like now, many decades ago it was the nerve center for one of the greatest operations in history.

The house has been kept nearly identical to the way it was during those few weeks that served as the turning point of World War II. In the center of the house lies the map room from which the final stages of the D-day invasion were planned. Today it sits empty; however, there's a hand-drawn picture hanging on the wall that shows what it looked like during the summer of 1944. Because the room was one of the most secret places in the world at the time, this picture, drawn from firsthand accounts, is the only visual reference of what it looked like back then.

In the picture, there are dozens of uniformed men and women packed into the room. Everyone has an exhausted and tense look on their faces. Maps cover every wall as well as the tables that have been pushed together to form a makeshift war room. At the front is a large painted map that depicts the English Channel, where a man on a ladder is moving wooden cutouts of ships. The operation was so secret that even this large map presented a challenge.

The Nazis knew an invasion was on the horizon and had developed a network of spies to uncover the details of the landing. The Allies, not having the time or manpower to build an accurate two-story map, hired a toy manufacturer to build it. Though it was a trusted company, the employees weren't cleared for the top-secret information. To not give away the precise location of the landings, a map of the entire European continent—the size of a large building—was commissioned. It was then shipped in sections, along with carpenters to assemble it. Once the carpenters arrived, however, they were instructed to only hang the section that depicted the Normandy coastline and then to burn the rest of the map. The carpenters, who now knew where the landing was taking place, were then placed under house arrest while a telegram was dispatched to their families informing them to not expect to hear from them for the foreseeable future.

In early June 1944, just days before the scheduled invasion, General Dwight D. Eisenhower, the Supreme Commander of the Allied forces, moved his headquarters into the house. The code name of the assault was Operation Overlord, and it was to be the largest in history. The numbers are overwhelming—1,200 aircraft, 5,000 ships, and over 160,000 troops would cross the English Channel in less than a day to dislodge the Nazis from the Normandy beaches. By the end of August, more than two million Allied troops were expected to have crossed into France.

The assault was just days away and was the culmination of over three years of intense planning. The international force consisted of thirteen nations, the majority being from the United States, the United Kingdom, and Canada. It had taken over two years just to manufacture, transport, and stockpile the necessary supplies for the operation—each soldier requiring ten tons of supplies and an additional ton for every month they were gone. To mask the precise landing point, a vast operation had been conducted to mislead the Germans, complete with fake radio traffic, fictitious army groups, and inflatable equipment. Even General Patton, perhaps the most feared military leader by the Germans, was enlisted to command a fake battalion and give credibility to the idea that the Allied invasion would be conducted hundreds of miles to the north at Pas-de-Calais. To further confuse the Germans, the famed counterintelligence agency MI5 had used a double agent to develop a ring of fictional spies, overwhelming German intelligence officers so completely that two armored divisions and nineteen infantry divisions were still held in reserve for months after D-day for the supposed "real" invasion.

The training and exercises leading up to D-day were unprecedented. A full live-fire rehearsal was carried out to train the American force landing on Utah Beach. Entire towns were evacuated for the weeklong drill, which included 30,000 troops and a three-mile-long armada of ships. During the first practice assault, a staggering 450 soldiers were killed just due to friendly fire. The preparation was deemed so important that the exercise continued. The following day, German E-boats then torpedoed and sank several of the landing ships, killing another 749 soldiers. After the incident, the Normandy invasion was nearly called off—not because of the loss of life but because there were rumors that German E-boats had hauled prisoners out of the water and were interrogating them. Several of the missing officers possessed above-top-secret, BIGOT (British Invasion of German Occupied Territory) level clearances, which put the invasion in jeopardy. For the next forty-eight hours, Navy divers combed the ocean floor until all of the officers' bodies were recovered. Everyone involved in the recovery was sworn to secrecy, and details of the event were kept sealed for nearly forty years.

With Eisenhower and his staff in place at Southwick

House, all of southern England was now one vast military camp. There were millions of soldiers cut off from the rest of the country by barbed wire and armed guards to prevent them from leaving and potentially leaking classified information. As Eisenhower described it, "A great human spring, coiled for the moment with its energy should be released and it would vault the English Channel in the greatest amphibious assault ever attempted."

Much of the planning was complete; however, it was up to Eisenhower to determine the go or no-go decision for the invasion, which was tentatively planned for the morning of June 5. Because moonlight was required for the airborne divisions and low tides were needed to carry out the landings, the Allies could only delay the operation until June 7, after which a minimum of two weeks would be required to regain the necessary conditions. However, a delay of that length would have cascading effects that would last for over a year and could jeopardize the Allied campaign.

Early on, Eisenhower had identified the most important variable to the operation as the unpredictable English weather. The month of May had been favorable; however, the weather in June was historically unstable and prone to rapid changes. The logistical challenge of unloading and attacking a fortified beach required ideal conditions. Low clouds would cause the paratroopers and gliders to miss their drop zones and would prevent Allied fighters carrying out close air support. Rough seas would mean many of the landing ships would sink before they made it to the beaches. Even if the initial wave was successful, a minimum of three days of good weather was needed to resupply the landing forces to sustain the expected German counterattack. The Allies had also built two enormous artificial harbors that needed to be towed into place to facilitate rapid offloading of cargo. The harbors alone consisted of over four hundred towed components and weighed more than twenty modern supercarriers. Towing them across the harbor and assembling the components required ideal conditions.

Eisenhower's weather office consisted of teams of experts from the British and American military as well as the national weather service. It was headed up by Royal Air Force Group Captain James Stagg, a veteran meteorologist who had led a polar expedition to the Arctic and who had served as the superintendent of London's famed Kew Observatory before being appointed as chief meteorological officer for Operation Overlord.

A large effort was underway to gather weather data for the operation—squadrons of stripped-down Halifax bombers were flying for hundreds of miles over the Atlantic, radioing back temperature and pressure movements. The ten-hour missions were being conducted around the clock despite the poor weather. Already, dozens of aircrews had been lost in the attempt to understand the weather movements to aid in Eisenhower's decision.

As the invasion drew to within seventy-two hours, Eisenhower began holding twice-a-day weather briefings in the house's library, a large beige room overlooking the grounds. The data so far had been inconclusive—there was a high-pressure system moving south from Iceland, causing pressure depressions over the Atlantic, typically a sign of poor weather. However, it was currently clear and favorable. Disagreements began to break out between the weather teams, which required Eisenhower's two-star chief of operations to intervene and say, "For heaven's sake, Stagg, get it sorted out by tomorrow morning before you come to the Supreme Commander's conference."

Although Operation Overlord was the largest invasion in history, there were still even larger geopolitical forces at work. Nearly six months prior, the three key Allied leaders of the war—Franklin Roosevelt, Winston Churchill, and Joseph Stalin—had met at a secret conference in Iran. The Russians had been fighting a brutal war of attrition on the eastern front, and Stalin was growing increasingly impatient with Roosevelt and Churchill. The Russians had so far caused 80 percent of German military casualties at the expense of a staggering twenty million casualties and nearly 40 percent of their country in ruin. As Russian commanders were fond of saying, they suffered more casualties before breakfast each morning than the Allies suffered in a month. And so, out of the conference, Roosevelt relented to Stalin's request for help and set a specific date for the invasion: May 1944.

In the months that followed, the initial invasion was expanded, causing the date to slip into early June. This frustrated the Russians, who were planning their own simultaneous attack on the eastern front. Because of the secrecy of the plan, they were only passed a tentative date of the end of May, with no additional details. Within Russia, there was growing skepticism that the whole plan was a deception by the U.S. and British, who never intended to hold up their end of the agreement.

The Allies, meanwhile, also feared a delay to the operation. It was becoming increasingly clear that once Germany fell, the Soviets would soon become an adversary. A successful campaign across France and into Germany would give the Allies far greater influence toward the reconstruction of Europe after the war.

By the evening of June 3, many of the ships were already underway in anticipation of the attack. The force was so large and the plan so complex that it had to be set in motion well before Eisenhower made his decision. During the nightly meeting, Stagg presented the weather, going on to say, "In all the charts for the forty or fifty years I had examined, I could not recall one which at this time of the year resembled this chart in the number and intensity of the depressions it portrayed at one time."

It was somehow a winter weather pattern but in the middle of the summer. To further add to the confusion, the weather was currently perfect outside. Staggs, however, stood by his forecast that it would soon change, with winds over forty-five miles per hour along with cloud cover that was under one thousand feet. Eisenhower went around the room polling his three top commanders. His naval commander recommended against proceeding—the initial assault could make it, but they wouldn't be able to resupply them, leaving the force exposed to a German counterattack. His air commander also recommended against proceeding—the low cloud cover would prevent the pilots from seeing their targets and distinguishing them from friendly forces. Only the ground commander wanted to continue with the operation. There was still a chance the weather would improve by the next morning, so

Eisenhower ordered everyone to reconvene the next day for a final decision.

At 4:30 the next morning, with the sky clear and the wind calm, Eisenhower asked Stagg if he foresaw a change. "No change, sir," he replied, going on to say that despite the current conditions being ideal, cloud cover was due to roll in over the next few hours. Eisenhower's ground commander still advocated to proceed with the operation, while the air commander advised to postpone it. The naval commander, meanwhile, reminded the men that with his armada already underway, they only had thirty minutes before they would cross the point of no return. After spending several minutes in thought, Eisenhower spoke. "Compared with the enemy's forces," he said, "ours are not overwhelmingly strong, we need every help our air superiority can give us. If the air cannot operate, we must postpone. Are there any dissentient votes?" Around the room none were given, so Eisenhower officially postponed the invasion.

Immediately, the commanders cleared the room to pull back their forces. Most of the ships and landing craft received the message and began sailing back to their harbors and ocean rendezvous points. However, a large formation of 138 ships didn't acknowledge the message and continued steaming toward Normandy. Radio operators desperately tried to contact them—if the ships didn't immediately turn around, it would be a disaster. The secrecy of the invasion would be lost, and the ships, without protection, would be easy prey for the Germans. However, there was no response from the ships as they continued sailing toward the coastline. Finally, a British Walrus biplane was dispatched to make contact. After several passes and multiple attempts to reach the ships, the pilot, as a last resort, dropped a canister on the deck of the lead ship with a written note informing the captain of the postponement. The task force finally reversed course, narrowly averting disaster.

By late morning, the clouds that Stagg had predicted arrived, turning the sky a dark gray. Eisenhower paced outside with one hand buried in his jacket pocket and the other continuously holding a lit cigarette. The forecast was now grim—the weather was expected to get significantly worse, ruling out an invasion for the next several days. A high-risk daylight landing on the eighth or ninth was possible; however, favorable tide and moon conditions would require a two-week postponement. That long of a delay would give the Germans more time to reinforce the beach and to deploy additional secret weapons, such as the feared V-1 rocket. Meanwhile, hundreds of thousands of troops would have to disembark and return to their camps, prolonging the tension and reducing morale. There was also a high risk to the secrecy of the operation with many troops now knowing the specifics of the plan. In addition, the issue of the Russians and the cascading effects weighed on him. As he was later described, Eisenhower was "bowed down with worry . . . as though each of the four stars on either shoulder weighed a ton."

In the evening, Eisenhower and his commanders met in the library with heavy rain beating on the windows and the wind howling outside. Stagg had a surprising new development—there was a small cold front west of Ireland that was due to move into Normandy on the morning of the sixth, which had the potential to create fair conditions for up to thirty-six hours. The seas would still be choppy, but the cloud cover might lift, allowing aerial and naval bombardment. The commanders discussed their options. The air commander hedged his advice by calling the decision to go "chancy," but possible. The naval commander thought the landing craft would have an inconvenient time of making it ashore but that it wouldn't be chaotic. He warned that many of the landing craft were now low on fuel, and if forced to abort again, they would need to return to port to refuel, a lengthy and complicated process. The ground commander said he was still a go—the Germans, lulled by their less accurate forecasts due to their smaller weather team, would likely have missed the break in weather and would be caught off guard.

For the next several minutes, the room went silent. Eisenhower pondered the decision, saying, to no one in particular, "The question is just how long can you keep this operation on the end of a limb and let it hang there." Still more silence. Finally, Eisenhower said, "I am quite positive we must give the order. I don't like it, but there it is." He gave a provisional go to the operation with the final decision to be made early the next morning.

Throughout the night, the storm grew worse. As Eisenhower described it:

"At 3:30 the next morning our little camp was shaking and shuddering under a wind of almost hurricane proportions and the accompanying rain seemed to be traveling in horizontal streaks. The mile-long trip through the muddy roads to the naval headquarters was anything but a cheerful one, since it seemed impossible that in such conditions there was any reason for even discussing the situation."

It was now the morning of June 5, the original planned invasion date. If the operation hadn't been postponed, the ships, after crossing turbulent seas, would have be approaching the Normandy coastline. A significant portion of the landing fleet would have already capsized and sunk, causing thousands to drown. The storms would have grounded the paratroopers and gliders, exposing the Allied flanks. Air support would have been nonexistent. Any attempt to have landed on June 5 would have been a catastrophic defeat for the Allies.

The commanders arrived at the house just after 4:00 a.m., bundled in overcoats to protect them from the horizontal sheets of rain. In the library, Stagg briefed the somber group that he had no significant changes to his forecast. As Eisenhower later wrote, "The prospect was not bright because of the possibility that we might land the first several waves successfully and then find later build-up impracticable, and so have to leave the isolated original attacking forces easy prey to the German counteraction."

As one of the commanders described, "Eisenhower got up from his chair and walked slowly up and down the room. . . . His head was slightly sunk on his chest, his hands clasped behind his back. From time to time, he stopped in his stride, turned his head quickly and jerkily in the direction of one of those present, and fired a rapid question at him . . . then resumed his walk."

There was still time to postpone the invasion. The Allies were betting everything on this operation. Three years of planning, two years of buildup, and hundreds of thousands of lives hung in the balance. An amphibious assault would not allow for an orderly retreat if they couldn't hold the beaches—the cost of failure would be massive. There was also the possibility that the United States, who was simultaneously fighting the Japanese in the Pacific, would shift their support away from Europe. The decision to proceed rested entirely with Eisenhower, which would later shock many of the German senior leaders, who would have never dared to make a decision of that magnitude without consulting Hitler.

As the storm continued to buffet the house, Eisenhower sat down on a sofa, where he pondered the decision for several minutes. Finally, Eisenhower spoke. "Well, Stagg," he said, "if this forecast comes off, I promise you we'll have a celebration when the time comes." He then said, "Okay, we'll go." With those three words, the invasion was now irrevocably set—the greatest invasion force in history had just been launched and would soon be put to the test. The room quickly cleared out as his commanders began relaying his decision to their subordinates.

After making one of the most important decisions in history, Eisenhower then shifted his focus toward mentally recovering. He no doubt had hundreds of smaller tasks that he could have attended to, but he knew that his decision-making would soon be called on again. Instead of focusing on less important tasks, he embraced the uncertainty and actively found ways to prevent himself from working.

After the meeting, Eisenhower sat down for breakfast and coffee. After a quick trip to the nearby harbor to see off the last embarking British divisions, he returned to play his aide in checkers and the board game Hounds and Fox. As his aide describes it:

"He won consistently, there being a trick in being a hound.

We played a game of cracker box checkers, and just as I had him cornered with my two kings and his one remaining king, damned if he didn't jump one of my kings and get a draw. At lunch we talked of old political yarns, he having known my old friend Pat Harrison when he was coming up as a young Congressman. . . . We talked on Senators and skunks and civet cats."

After lunch, Eisenhower then sat down and wrote a note that was found by an aide weeks later in a wastebasket:

> Our landings in the Cherbourg-Havre area have failed to gain a satisfactory foothold and I have withdrawn the troops. My decision to attack at this time and place was based upon the best information available. The troops, the air and the Navy did all that Bravery and devotion to duty could do. If any blame or fault attaches to the attempt, it is mine alone.

Fortunately, Eisenhower never had to send the letter. The results have been well documented—the Germans didn't see the break in the weather and were caught completely by surprise. Within twenty-four hours, the Allies had gained a tenuous foothold that they gradually expanded. Within months, they were able to liberate Paris, and within the year drove back the Germans, eventually resulting in the destruction of the Nazi regime.

PRIORITIZE

Eisenhower made one of the best decisions in history, in large part because of his ability to prioritize. "What is important is seldom urgent and what is urgent is seldom important," he would often say. Some tasks are urgent—if they're not completed within a given time frame, the opportunity is gone. Others are important; the consequences of getting them right are high. By breaking down tasks according to their importance and urgency, he was able to develop a simple but effective framework for prioritizing his time and energy, allowing him to focus on making the best decision possible.

TIME ALLOCATION

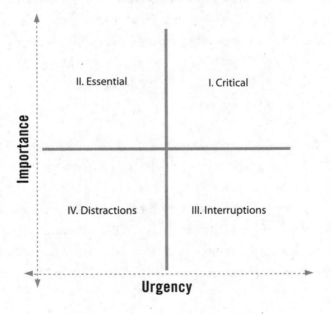

The technique can be visualized as a graph with importance on the vertical axis and urgency on the horizontal axis, forming four quadrants. In the upper-right corner, quadrant

I, we have the urgent *and* important. These are the critical action items that need to be done immediately. As fighter pilots, we call these *near rocks*—things ahead that could potentially kill us. They're the decisions that have to do with the safety and well-being of friendly forces, civilians, or ourselves. If the cockpit is filling with smoke, for instance, stopping the smoke takes precedence over everything else. When we're planning missions, an airborne tanker falling out at the last minute requires an immediate decision as to whether there is enough fuel to complete the mission. For a software developer, it could be a security breach, or as a physician, it could be a patient having a heart attack. Energy and resources need to be immediately prioritized toward resolving the situation. However, it's important to note that decisions and tasks are not evenly distributed across the quadrants. If properly planned, only a small percentage of tasks should fall into this quadrant.

In the upper-left quadrant, quadrant II, are important decisions and tasks but ones that aren't urgent. These are essential to complete but don't have an immediate deadline. For fighter pilots, they are called *far rocks*—things that will become a factor within the next several minutes. When mission planning, these are potential blockers that may impede overall mission success. For a health administrator, this would be ensuring that your facilities have the necessary resources to operate properly. For a civil engineer, this would be ensuring the projects are being completed safely. The key to quadrant II tasks is spending time to develop a road map and scheduling it early so that it doesn't fall out of your cross-check and eventually turn into a quadrant I task.

When Eisenhower arrived at Southwick House, he identified the launch decision as the most important call he had to make. With most of the planning done, almost all his effect on the operation came down to when he chose to execute. He was no doubt inundated with hundreds of other requests during his time there, but none of them came close to the importance of delaying the invasion on the first attempt, and then, with the break in the weather, executing on the second attempt.

In the lower-right quadrant, quadrant III, there are tasks that are urgent but not important. This is where the brilliance of Eisenhower's system starts to shine. Most people understand and, for the most part, adhere to the previous quadrants naturally. However, what should be prioritized: A task that's urgent or one that's important? Logically, it should be the important task, but psychologically, we're often drawn into completing the urgent task because of what's known as the *urgency effect*. This is why we often get sucked into email and work chats at the expense of deep work and the deliberate practice that's necessary for accomplishing a long-term goal. It's where interruptions from coworkers and unnecessary meetings live. Unfortunately, as our world becomes more digital, the problem's only getting worse—the barrage of email and other notifications provide an attention slot machine for our brains, which are wired for novelty and easily get sidetracked. Combined with our desire to feel busy and productive, it's easy to get sucked into this quadrant. However, it's been shown that if attention is brought to the potential outcomes *before* making a decision, the effect is diminished. That's why it is necessary to classify tasks according to which quadrant they belong in before starting on them—the act forces the brain to factor in the long-term implications instead of defaulting to what's urgent.

Eisenhower's solution for quadrant III tasks was to delegate them—if they needed to be done but they didn't require his specific skill set, he would find someone else who could do them. For many, this is one of the most difficult skills to learn. As a fighter pilot, after several years of flying as a wingman, where your job is to do the tedious work, such as loading the mission files into the jet, preparing the briefing rooms, and being on call to assist senior pilots, you eventually go through an upgrade to become a flight lead in charge of several other aircraft. The skills required to lead formations of aircraft are different from the skills required to be a wingman. A four-ship of modern fighters is a strategic resource that can swing the tide of a battle. As a flight lead, you need to understand the big picture, think at a high level, and communicate your intent to the rest of your formation so they can then carry out your vision. However, after several years of serving as a wingman, many new flight leads struggle with this and get sucked into the smaller tasks that they're familiar with. This prevents them from seeing the big picture and often leads to mission failure. The solution is to understand that you can't do it all and that, as a flight lead, you need to off-load tasks to your wingmen so that you can free up mental bandwidth for the things only you can do (quadrant II decisions). The same concept applies outside of the cockpit—we have a limited amount of time and energy and need to apply it to the most important tasks to achieve our long-term goals. While many people don't have teams to help them carry out quadrant III tasks, technology is increasingly filling the gap. Scheduling software, automated financing, and emails sorted and filtered by AI are now readily accessible to anyone with a smartphone. Investing our time by learning how to leverage technology can allow us to stay focused on what's important.

Quadrant IV is comprised of distractions that aren't important or urgent. These are time-wasting tasks that should be cut entirely. If they don't in some way contribute to your long-term goals and aren't something you'll get penalized for failing to do, then they shouldn't be a part of your task list. The principle here is that the fastest process is no process at all.

Tasks in quadrant IV are different from leisure time, which consists of things you *want* to do that will mentally and physically recharge yourself. Some were likely surprised that Eisenhower was playing board games during the D-day invasion. However, understanding yourself and when to step away to recharge is a critical step in making good decisions. While I was in combat, our sorties would sometimes last eight hours, which is a long time to be continually making decisions. To mentally recharge, I would take a few sips of water every fifteen minutes and have a few bites of food every hour. It wasn't much, but it allowed me to extend my focus for longer periods of time.

The most important underlying question when prioritizing is: What are we working toward? Without clear objectives or goals, it's difficult to understand how everything fits together. If there isn't a clear vision, our minds will default toward urgent tasks, whether they're important or not. It's only by staying disciplined toward that vision that we can ruthlessly cut tasks that don't matter and maximize our impact.

BAGRAM

As the engine in my F-16 continued to spool up, the rusted-out fuel truck continued barreling toward my aircraft. There have been times in my career where I felt fear, but it was completely absent now—just an overwhelming curiosity as to how the situation would turn out. It was like watching a movie that was playing out, only I was in it. Time seemed to slow down as all external thoughts disappeared—everything was slowly unfolding in front of me. My crew chief, keying his mic, asked, "What should we do?"

Based off intelligence reports and what had already occurred throughout the day, I estimated there was a fifty-fifty chance that this was another suicide bomber. Despite the stakes being high, the answer was simple. A fully loaded fuel truck can carry nearly forty thousand pounds of fuel—which, if detonated, would make it one of the largest conventional bombs in the world. I was also sitting on top of a fully fueled jet and carrying an assortment of bombs, missiles, and bullets, which in turn was parked next to several other F-16s. If this was a suicide bomber, none of us were going to survive the blast. Conversely, if it wasn't a suicide bomber, then we would still need to carry out our mission.

I keyed the mic to our operations center. Typically, as a fighter pilot, you want to speak in a low, calm voice when talking on the radio so that you can be a calming force for others. In this case, I wanted to convey a sense of urgency, so I increased the pacing and harshness of my voice and said, "There's an unidentified suspicious truck moving rapidly toward the F-16 ramp. We need it secured now."

The truck came to a stop several dozen feet from my jet, the air brakes letting out a hiss as the suspension rocked back and forth. The cabin was dark as it sat there in the shadow of the white security lights. This was the moment of truth. What was going to happen next? It was impossible to not slightly tense up in anticipation for what might happen; however, there wasn't time to sit there and watch—I had made the decision to continue the start, so my crew chief and I continued the sequence as quickly as possible. Out of the corner of my eye, I could see people pouring from an adjacent bunker, wearing T-shirts and armed with rifles. They weren't security forces but were maintainers. Despite not having the training, I watched as ten of them sprinted toward the truck with their M16s. They climbed up on it, ripped open the door, and dragged out the driver.

By this point, the F-16 was now capable of taxiing. My objective was to get my wingman and my jet out of harm's way in case there was a remote detonator on the truck. At least we would have two F-16s operational and airborne to help secure the base from an attack. I pushed the throttle up, taxied clear, and took off on the mission.

Once we took off, the maintainers secured the area and set up a perimeter while waiting for security forces. Once they arrived, they took the driver into custody. They never were able to figure out if he had malicious intent or not. He had originated from a foreign area of the base and wasn't authorized to be in the area. No explosives were found; however, it was speculated that he may have been attempting to ram one of the jets but changed his mind at the last minute. All told, five U.S. personnel were lost that day, with another seventeen injured.

DECISIVE

People often struggle at being decisive and taking action, particularly as the stakes are raised. They overthink the problem and tie up their mental bandwidth trying to make the perfect decision. Combined with the body's physiological reaction to stress and pressure, this can lead to confusion and an inability to be decisive.

When I fly with new students, it's easy for them to become task saturated. Learning how to fly a fighter is difficult—there are thousands of commands that connect the pilot to the aircraft. It's like speaking a new language, and it takes several years to become fluent in it. Combined with their motivation to succeed, this often leads them to mentally overreach. What I tell them is to never let yourself get more than 90 percent task saturated. You need bandwidth to see the big picture and prioritize the list of never-ending tasks. Once you let yourself get 100 percent task saturated, you're no longer in control—tasks will automatically start dropping off, whether you want them to or not, and you won't be able to triage the situation properly.

The solution is simple, but difficult to execute—they need

to do *less*. Once you're approaching 90 percent capacity, you need to smartly shed tasks. You may want to do more, others may want you to do more, but the best thing you can do is to understand your limitations and communicate them effectively. The lesson is not just for students, though. As you become more experienced as a fighter pilot, the novelty and excitement decrease and you become a more effective and lethal fighter pilot. However, for even experienced fighter pilots, there are edge cases where you can easily slip into being task saturated. One of them is when you hear friendly forces are under fire and you have an opportunity to help them. Every ounce of you wants to save them as quickly as possible. It's important, though, to forgo the temptation to rush—stay at the 90 percent level, because those troops need a clear, decisive thinker overhead.

Another reason people are indecisive is because they struggle to remove all uncertainty from decisions. The best decision-makers meet uncertainty with a smile. There are very few opportunities in life where you can be 100 percent sure in your decision. While there are tools, such as fast-forecasting, to help remove some uncertainty, ultimately, we're just trying to tip the odds of a positive outcome in our favor as much as possible. Every moment you're not making a decision is a cost that you're incurring in terms of time and mental energy. Eventually, that cost will overwhelm the benefit of waiting—that's the point where it's time to make a decision and move on.

Another way to look at decision-making is that we're just trying to remove the choices that are clearly not optimal.

Imagine mapping a thousand different routes across your town to a specific destination; 99 percent of those routes are going to clearly be poor choices. Those are easy to eliminate, likely leaving you with a few good options. Based off your priorities—minimal time, minimal complexity, minimal fuel, best scenery—you can also eliminate some of the remaining choices, leaving you with just two or three options. This is the point where a lot of people get stuck. They continue to try to refine their assessment until they only have one option left. However, there's often either too much uncertainty or the options are too different to come up with just one choice. Instead of continuing to deliberate, the solution is now simple: Go with any of the remaining viable options. Your energy and time are better spent on a different problem or remaining flexible for the likely adjustments you'll have to make due to something unforeseen. If still in doubt, go with the simplest option—that will allow you to save mental energy while also minimizing the points of failure when carrying it out.

For life decisions, I found that when there are multiple seemingly equal choices, going with the riskiest viable option usually provides the greatest return in value. Most people hate uncertainty, particularly when it's combined with risk. As humans, we are biologically programmed to overestimate risk. If you're able to overcome that mental hurdle, it becomes easy to differentiate yourself and greatly increase your odds of success.

Now, if at this point, you're still in doubt, I'll share a trick I learned as a child for deciding between several equal choices. Stick out a finger—one for each viable option. Then hit them on a solid surface and whichever one you can feel the most, go with that one. Of course, it's clearly better if you can use critical thinking to narrow the choices down to one option; however, when you're stuck and running out of time, give it a shot.

AFTERWORD

B
eing able to consistently make good decisions is one of the great challenges of our time. We are living through a technological revolution that's fundamentally altering the way we live, work, and relate to one another. Whereas the nineteenth and twentieth centuries were primarily focused on the effects of the Industrial Revolution and how to manage large groups of people, this century's leaders will be defined by how clearly they think and make decisions.

Already, artificial intelligence and other technological aids are augmenting and, in many cases, replacing the rote and repetitive work in our lives. Like revolutions that preceded it, this revolution is disrupting nearly every industry across the world—everything from how we plan our travel, to how we work, to how we raise our children is changing. This is leading to an increasingly dynamic environment where decisions can't be made the same way they've always been made—decisions need to be continually reassessed, often at breakneck speeds.

However, for those who can adapt, this technological leverage is allowing them to produce far greater results than anything they could have achieved in the past.

The key to unlocking this power is through clear decision-making—finding a deliberate and iterative way of making decisions that produces the best value based on the given constraints. As fighter pilots, we've been undergoing this revolution for several decades, and this book represents many of the principles that we've learned for thriving in a complex and dynamic environment filled with uncertainty. Already, these lessons have been implemented by surgeons, professional coaches, CIA agents, CEOs, NASA astronauts, and many others who we've trained over the years.

The ability to clearly assess a problem, generate potential courses of action, assess expected value, and then execute is a universal skill that everyone can learn and improve upon. This book represents a starting point and shouldn't be used as dogma. Knowledge is only useful to the degree that it can be drawn upon and used when it's needed. It doesn't matter how well the information can be recalled in a sterile environment—the only thing that matters is how well it can be used in the real world, where there are distractions, uncertainties, and risks. The lessons in this book *will* make you a better decision-maker, but now the real work begins: finding a way to seamlessly integrate these concepts into the mental framework that you've accumulated throughout your lifetime. Good luck.

ACKNOWLEDGMENTS

This book, over six years in the making, is my attempt to pass along the knowledge and wisdom that I've learned during my career as a fighter pilot. Any errors or issues that are found are solely my responsibility.

Above all, I would like to acknowledge my family for their unwavering support while not just writing this book but throughout my life. Long days of training, short-notice trips, and flying into combat are things I volunteered for, but for my family, these are burdens they inherited. Every time a jet went down, it was my family who had to wait and see if their husband, father, son, or brother had been lost.

In the writing of this book, my wife, Kylie, deserves special recognition. For over a year and a half she enabled me to write every single day. During that period, she was the only person I trusted to read the raw, unedited text, providing continual feedback and support. I would also like to thank my children not only for the time they gave me to write but for allowing me to witness their insatiable curiosity and love of learning, which has taught me far more than I've taught them.

I would like to thank my parents, Ping and Deborah, who nurtured and supported a kid with more than a streak of rebelliousness. As a child, I did not make their lives easy. However, their ample patience and guidance allowed me to eventually harness that power. The same goes for my siblings, Derek and Sophia, who have dedicated their lives to service.

I would also like to recognize my good friend Dan Schilling, a former combat controller and now author, for advising me throughout the writing process as well as introducing me to my agent, Larry Weissman. Larry deserves great credit for his many hours working with me and how he sprung to life with a killer instinct worthy of a fighter pilot when finding a publisher.

My editor, Marc Resnick, also deserves recognition. His calming demeanor and unwavering confidence in my writing allowed me to shape this book into what you see today. The same goes for the rest of the St. Martin's Press team, who provided a significant amount of support.

Lastly, I would like to express gratitude to my fellow fighter pilots: These warriors of the sky have dedicated a tremendous amount of blood, sweat, and tears over the years, forming the United States military into the most formidable fighting force in the world. Few will ever truly understand how large of an impact this small group has made in defending freedom. On a personal level, their continual guidance and support during my career helped shape me into the man I am today. The same goes for the writing of this book: Many current and former fighter pilots have helped hone the concepts and writing within these pages. Some have since flown west . . . Crush 'Em, AFF, Prowl, Banzai, Strength and Honor. . . .

BIBLIOGRAPHY

INTRODUCTION

"Fatal Airliner (14+ Passengers) Hull-Loss Accidents." *Aviation Safety Network*, Flight Safety Foundation, https://aviation-safety.net/statistics/period /stats.php?cat=A. Archived from the original on July 26, 2012, https://web .archive.org/web/20120726023922/http:/aviationsafety.net/statistics/period /stats.php?cat=A1. Retrieved December 21, 2012.

"Global Fatal Accident Review 2002 to 2011." *UK Civil Aviation Authority*, https://web.archive.org/web/20170802210140/http:/publicapps.caa.co.uk /docs/33/CAP%201036%20Global%20Fatal%20Accident%20Review%20 2002%20to%202011.pdf. Archived from the original on August 2, 2017, https:// www.gov.uk/government/organisations/civil-aviation-authority. Retrieved August 2, 2017.

CHAPTER 1: ASSESS

Armstrong, Paul. "Has Air France Flight 447 Mystery Finally Been Solved?" CNN, Cable News Network, July 5, 2012, https://www.cnn.com/2012/07/04 /world/europe/air-france-flight-447-explainer/index.html.

Faccini, Barbara. "Four Minutes, 23 Seconds." *Volare Aviation Monthly*, January 2013.

Irving, Clive. "Air France Flight 447 Crash Timeline." *The Daily Beast*, The

Daily Beast Company, July 13, 2017, https://www.thedailybeast.com/air-france-flight-447-crash-timeline.

O'Brien, Jamie. "Mystery Over the Atlantic: The Tragic Fate of Air France Flight 447." *The CASE Journal*, vol. 15, no. 1, 2019, pp. 22–45, https://doi.org/10.1108/tcj-08-2018-0090.

"Who We Are." *Airbus*, June 14, 2021, https://www.airbus.com/en/who-we-are.

CHAPTER 2: POWER LAWS

"Excite-Magellan Merger Signals Trend." CNET, June 29, 1996, https://www.cnet.com/tech/mobile/excite-magellan-merger-signals-trend/.

Fisk, Peter. "Metcalfe's Law Explains How the Value of Networks Grows Exponentially . . . Exploring the 'Network Effects' of Businesses Like Apple, Facebook, Trulia and Uber." March 18, 2020, https://www.peterfisk.com/2020/02/metcalfes-law-explains-how-the-value-of-networks-grow-exponentially-there-are-5-types-of-network-effects/.

Hewitt, Paul. "Exponential Growth and Doubling Time." *The Science Teacher*, August 2020.

Langhe, Bart de, et al. "Linear Thinking in a Nonlinear World." *Harvard Business Review*, June 2017.

Levy, Steven. *In the Plex: How Google Thinks, Works, and Shapes Our Lives.* 1st ed. New York: Simon & Schuster, 2011.

McCullough, Brian. "Excite.com CEO George Bell." *Internet History Podcast*, November 2014.

Peer, Eyal, and Eyal Gamliel. "Pace Yourself: Improving Time-Saving Judgment When Increasing Activity Speed." *PsycExtra Dataset*, 2012, https://doi.org/10.1037/e519682015-085.

Szekely, Pablo, et al. "The Mass-Longevity Triangle: Pareto Optimality and the Geometry of Life-History Trait Space." *PLOS Computational Biology*, vol. 11, no. 10, 2015, https://doi.org/10.1371/journal.pcbi.1004524.g004.

West, Geoffrey B. *Scale: The Universal Laws of Growth, Innovation, Sustainability, and the Pace of Life in Organisms, Cities, Economies, and Companies.* New York: Penguin Press, 2017.

Ziv, Shahar. "Which Would You Pick: $1,000,000 or a Magical Penny?" *Forbes*, December 10, 2021, https://www.forbes.com/sites/shaharziv/2019/07/30/can-you-correctly-answer-the-magical-penny-question/?sh=549eed6f1a64.

CHAPTER 3: LEARNED LESSONS

Boyne, Walter. "Red Flag." *Air & Space Forces*, November 2001.

Herculano-Houzel, Suzana, and Jon H. Kaas. "Gorilla and Orangutan Brains Conform to the Primate Cellular Scaling Rules: Implications for Human Evolution." *Brain, Behavior and Evolution*, vol. 77, no. 1, 2011, pp. 33–44, https://doi.org/10.1159/000322729.

Ridley, Matt. *The Rational Optimist: How Prosperity Evolves.* 1st U.S. ed. New York: Harper, 2010.

CHAPTER 4: FAST-FORECASTING

"How Many Calculations Per Second Can the Human Brain Do?" NeuroTray, October 19, 2022, https://neurotray.com/how-many-calculations-per-second-can-the-human-brain-do/.

"Nicholas Carr: 'Are We Becoming Too Reliant on Computers?'" *The Guardian*, January 17, 2015, https://www.theguardian.com/books/2015/jan/17/nicholas-carr-are-we-becoming-too-reliant-on-computers.

CHAPTER 5: CREATIVITY

Barnes, Julian E. "Why the U.S. Was Wrong About Ukraine and the Afghan War." *The New York Times*, March 24, 2022, https://www.nytimes.com/2022/03/24/us/politics/intelligence-agencies-ukraine-afghanistan.html.

Cohen, Eliot (ed.). *Gulf War Air Power Survey, Volume IV: Weapons, Tactics, and Training and Space Operations.* Washington, D.C.: Department of the Air Force, 1993.

Comer, Richard. "Operation Eager Anvil: Pave Low Leaders." *Defense Media Network*, https://www.defensemedianetwork.com/stories/operation-eager-anvil-pave-low-leaders/.

Deptula, David. "Effects-Based Operations: Change in the Nature of Warfare." *Aerospace Education Foundation*, February 2001.

Duczynski, Guy. *Effects-Based Operations: A Guide for Practitioners.* Perth, Australia: Edith Cowan University, 2004.

"Gulf War Fast Facts." CNN, Cable News Network, https://edition.cnn.com/2013/09/15/world/meast/gulf-war-fast-facts/index.html. Archived from the original on November 12, 2020, https://web.archive.org/web/20201112020744/https:/edition.cnn.com/2013/09/15/world/meast/gulf-war-fast-facts/index.html. Retrieved December 15, 2020.

Keeney, Ralph. "Creativity in Decision Making with Value-Focused Thinking." *MIT Sloan Management Review*, Summer 1994.

Mackenzie, Richard. "Apache Attack." *Air Force*, October 1991.

Rich, Ben R., and Leo Janos. *Skunk Works: A Personal Memoir of My Years at Lockheed*. 1st ed. New York: Little, Brown, 1994.

Underwood, Beth. "Blinding Saddam." *Military History*, March 2017.

Whitcomb, Darrel. "Flying the First Mission of Desert Storm." *Air Power History*, 2012.

CHAPTER 6: MENTAL TOUGHNESS

Arnsten, Amy F. "Stress Signalling Pathways That Impair Prefrontal Cortex Structure and Function." *Nature Reviews Neuroscience*, vol. 10, no. 6, 2009, pp. 410–422, https://doi.org/10.1038/nrn2648.

"Explosive Weapon Effects: Final Report," Geneva International Centre for Humanitarian Demining, Geneva, February 2017.

United States District Court, District of South Carolina, Greenville Division. *Winston Tyler Hencely vs. Fluor Corporation, Inc.; Fluor Enterprises, Inc.; Fluor Intercontinental, Inc.; Fluor Government Group International, Inc.*, June 2020.

CHAPTER 7: PRIORITIZE AND BE DECISIVE

Butcher, Harry. *My Three Years with Eisenhower*. New York: Simon and Schuster, 1946.

Buttle, Cameron. "The RAF Weathermen Who Helped Save D-Day." *BBC News*, British Broadcasting Corporation, June 4, 2019, https://www.bbc.com/news/uk-scotland-48498383.

D'Este, Carlo. "The Storm Before the Storm." HistoryNet, March 29, 2022, https://www.historynet.com/the-storm-before-the-storm/?f.

Eisenhower, David. *Eisenhower at War, 1943–1945*. 1st ed. New York: Random House, 1986.

Hand, Rodger. "'Okay, We'll Go'—An Analysis of Eisenhower's Decisions Launching Overlord." *Army History*, Spring 1997.

"How Busyness Leads to Bad Decisions." *BBC Worklife*, British Broadcast-

ing Corporation, https://www.bbc.com/worklife/article/20191202-how-time
-scarcity-makes-us-focus-on-low-value-tasks.

Sibbons, Mike. *From the Archives: An Eclectic Mix of Stories from the History
of REME*. Oxford: Osprey Publishing, 2016.

ABOUT THE AUTHOR

Hasard X

Hasard Lee is a U.S Air Force fighter pilot who began his career flying the F-16. As a flight commander he led pilots into combat during one of the most intense periods during the War in Afghanistan. There he flew over eighty combat missions and became the only fighter pilot to ever fly two different types of jets into combat on the same day while supporting troops under fire.

Hasard was then handpicked to fly the F-35—the most advanced and expensive weapons system in history—which was still in development at the time. During his last role on active duty, Hasard became the Chief of Training Systems for the largest training base in the world, leading the development of new technology and teaching methods to train future fighter pilots. Hasard speaks and consults for organizations. His social media accounts reach over 290 million people annually. *The Art of Clear Thinking* is his first book.